RACE TO ZERO

Marian Krüger
Benedict Probst

in collaboration with
Sebastian Hanss-Mirodone

RACE TO ZERO

How Companies Can Lead
the Way to Climate Neutrality

Campus Verlag
Frankfurt/New York

The original German edition was published in 2024
by Campus Verlag GmbH with the title *Race to Zero –
Wie Unternehmen den Wettlauf zur Klimaneutralität gewinnen.*
© 2024 by Campus Verlag GmbH. All rights reserved.

ISBN 978-3-593-52065-0 Print
ISBN 978-3-593-46143-4 E-Book (PDF)
ISBN 978-3-593-46142-7 E-Book (EPUB)

All rights reserved. No part of this book may be reproduced or transmitted
in any form or by any means, electronic or mechanical, including photocopying,
recording, or by any information storage and retrieval system, without
permission in writing from the publishers.
Copyright © 2025 Campus Verlag, part of Verlagsgruppe Beltz,
Werderstr. 10, 69469 Weinheim, info@campus.de.
Cover design: www.studioheyhey.com
Interior illustrations: © Lorna Schütte, Berlin (lornaschuette.com)
Typesetting: Publikations Atelier, Weiterstadt
Set in Scala and URW DIN
Printing office and bookbinder: Beltz Grafische Betriebe GmbH, Bad Langensalza
Beltz Grafische Betriebe is a climate-neutral company (ID 15985-2104-1001)
Printed in Germany

www.campus.de
www.press.uchicago.edu

FOR OUR FAMILIES

CONTENTS

PREFACE 11

I THE RACE TO NET ZERO

1 THE PATH TO NET ZERO 19
    The World of Tomorrow 22
    Net Zero? 25
    What Makes an Ambitious Climate Target? 26
    The Race to Zero with SBTi 29
    SBTi is Not Perfect 32
    Why Some U.S. Companies
    Are Still Struggling with SBTi 34

2 THE CARBON CREDIT JUNGLE 37
    How the Voluntary Carbon Market Came to Be 40
    How Carbon Crediting Projects Work 43
    What Is Going Wrong in the Voluntary Carbon Market? . 45
    Different Types of Credits 48
    Carbon Credits for Net Zero 50
    To Achieve Net Zero, We Need Carbon Removal 52
    The Way Forward 54

II CARBON REMOVAL

3 OVERVIEW OF THE MOST IMPORTANT CARBON REMOVAL METHODS 59
  One World, Two Cycles 60

4 LETTING NATURE DO THE HEAVY LIFTING 65
  Afforestation/Reforestation 66
  Regenerative Agriculture 72
  Peatlands 80
  Biomass Conservation 83
  Blue Carbon 87

5 LENDING NATURE A HELPING HAND 95
  Enhanced Weathering 97
  Ocean Alkalinity Enhancement 104
  Biochar Carbon Removal 112

6 ENGINEERED SOLUTIONS FROM BIOENERGY TO CO_2 SCRUBBERS . 123
  Bioenergy with Carbon Capture and Storage 124
  Direct Air Carbon Capture and Storage 131
  CO_2 Storage I – Geological 138
  CO_2 Storage II – In Products 144

III FIRST STEPS

7 HOW DO I GET GOING? 153
  Diversifiers and Purists 155
  Key Principles for Making Purchases 158
  Decision-Making Framework 160
  How to Get Going 164
  Communication Is Key 166

8	**SECURE, FAIR AND AFFORDABLE CARBON REMOVAL – BEYOND THE COMPANY**	169
	How We Can Make Carbon Removal Safe	172
	How We Can Make Carbon Removal Fair	176
	How We Can Make Carbon Removal Affordable	181

EPILOGUE 187
    A Long Road Ahead 190
    Outlook 191
    Global Justice 194

ACKNOWLEDGMENTS 197

SOURCES 199

ABOUT THE AUTHORS 223

PREFACE

> "The future is already here,
> it's just not evenly distributed."
>
> William Gibson, science fiction author

The Head of Sustainability at a well-known company runs her fingers through her hair, the stress evident in every line of her face. In just a few days, she has to present the company's climate strategy to the board, but there's one nagging issue she just can't seem to crack: those emissions that can't be reduced to zero. How should the company deal with these residual emissions in the long term? There are plenty of cheap options out there – like carbon credits from tropical forest conservation projects. But she's not convinced. "Can we really trust these to offset our emissions?" she asks us.

Her skepticism isn't misplaced. Carbon credits have taken quite a beating in recent years, and she's understandably worried about the company's reputation. No one wants to end up as part of a *Bloomberg* headline like: "Delta and Credit Suisse claim carbon neutrality using junk carbon offsets." That would be a PR nightmare. But at first glance, it's tempting to outsource the problem to an external company and let them offset these residual emissions. Voilà – carbon neutrality on a budget, without the headaches, and with a glossy marketing campaign featuring lush, green rainforests.

Other companies share the same concerns as our Head of Sustainability. Over the past years, we've fielded questions from a wide range of organizations, all grappling with how to achieve net zero – that elusive point where they no longer emit more greenhouse gases than they actively remove from the atmosphere. While some companies have clear guidelines from initiatives like the Science Based Targets initiative (SBTi) to reduce their direct emissions, figuring out what to do with the remaining emissions remains a challenge for many.

Leaders like Microsoft are setting ambitious examples. By 2030, the American tech giant plans to cross the net zero threshold through a combination of CO_2 reduction and removal strategies. And they're not stopping there – Microsoft aims to remove all of its historical emissions from the atmosphere. Similar plans, but on a smaller scale, have been put in place by Stripe, McKinsey, and Shopify. Individually or collectively, these companies have developed standards for offsetting their remaining emissions. While Microsoft currently leads the way as one of the largest buyers of carbon credits, its commitments should be taken with a grain of salt, as its carbon footprint has recently increased significantly with the expansion of AI technologies. Building data centers and running AI models requires significant resources

Unlike these frontrunners, not every company has the luxury of a dedicated team to navigate the carbon credit landscape. The voluntary carbon markets can feel like a dense jungle, teeming with credits from projects ranging from forest protection in Brazil to energy-efficient cookstoves in Kenya and renewable energy initiatives in China.

In addition, we've seen the emergence of novel technologies designed to tackle the challenge of removing carbon from the atmosphere and storing it durably. Unlike traditional methods such as forest conservation or renewable energy projects, which focus on preventing emissions that would otherwise be released, these approaches remove emissions that already entered the atmosphere.

Think of it as giving the atmosphere a much-needed deep clean. There's a wide range of such options, from biochar to enhanced weathering. But with that variety comes a plethora of price points and a fair share of scientific uncertainties, particularly around how safe and scalable these new methods are. If these terms are completely new to you, don't worry, we've got you covered.

Over the past few years, we've been helping companies and journalists alike navigate the often-confusing world of net zero. We're Marian and Ben, by the way. Marian is the co-founder and director of the nonprofit organization remove, which supports startups in Europe and the Global South aiming to remove harmful greenhouse gases like CO_2 from the atmosphere. Ben runs the Net Zero Lab at the Max Planck Institute for Innovation and Competition in Munich and has years of experience studying carbon markets and corporate climate strategies.

We first crossed paths while working in Professor Volker Hoffmann's Group for Sustainability and Technology at ETH Zurich, Switzerland's premier research university. It didn't take long for us to realize that we had complementary skills. With his entrepreneurial background, Marian is deeply rooted in the European and global startup scene. At the same time, Ben has a deep understanding of the policy and corporate frameworks that will shape how businesses navigate their journey to net zero. But perhaps the most important reason we clicked: We both genuinely enjoy this work.

In all our conversations with companies, one thing has become very clear – many businesses are taking the climate crisis seriously and are eager to make a difference. This shift is evident in the ambitious climate targets being set across the board. By August 2024, over 5,800 companies had set ambitious climate targets with guidance from the Science Based Targets initiative (SBTi). SBTi was created to help companies align their business strategies with the goals of the Paris Climate Agreement, ensuring that their targets are based on science.

Under the SBTi framework, companies can only claim true carbon neutrality if they've slashed at least 90 percent of their emissions and neutralized the remaining amount through durable carbon removal. With such stringent criteria, it's no surprise that we don't know of any companies that have fully achieved net zero under these standards.

Not every company has jumped on the SBTi bandwagon or committed to strict net zero targets. Some have taken a different route, making a splash with high-profile marketing campaigns. These days, you'll find a lot of products labeled as carbon neutral. While everyone's talking about carbon neutral driving and flying, some brands have taken it a step further, offering "climate-positive" baby food. That's right – baby food that's not only good for little tummies but supposedly good for the planet, too.

But how real are these claims? A revealing investigation by *The Guardian* shed light on the dangers of these half-hearted climate strategies. Major companies such as Gucci and Nestlé bought carbon credits from forest protection projects to market their products as carbon neutral. The problem? Many of these forest projects didn't actually protect any forests. Meanwhile, these companies continued to emit CO_2, banking on the illusion of carbon neutrality. The "carbon neutral" label has since disappeared from Nestlé's KitKat and Nespresso capsules.

Whether companies claim to have ambitious climate targets or are already touting "carbon neutrality" through clever marketing, the reality is that political and economic pressures are closing in. The EU, for example, is currently working on standards that will shape what climate claims companies can make in the future. Ambitious climate policies in Europe and beyond will affect every business – whether they like it or not. So, wouldn't it make more sense to be proactive now?

These questions and concerns inspired us to write this book. In addition to our own research, we spoke to more than 40 experts to explore how companies can truly succeed in the race to net zero. We pay particular attention to the "negative" side of net zero – how companies should neutralize any residual emissions by removing carbon from the atmosphere. While reduction strategies will vary widely across companies and industries, the approach to securing negative emissions will be strikingly similar, regardless of sector.

Our goal with this book is to demystify the murky waters of carbon markets, introduce some of the pioneers in carbon removal, and highlight the potential benefits and risks for companies. We've focused on CO_2 because it makes up the majority of greenhouse gases. We recognize that other greenhouse gases, such as methane, also play a critical role, but diving into those would take us too far.

In the first part of this book, we look at the best frameworks for crafting corporate climate strategies. We'll also explore what's going wrong and what companies can learn from the pitfalls and scandals of the current voluntary carbon market. In the second part, we introduce new options for climate offsetting: negative emissions, also known as carbon removal. Finally, in part three, we discuss how companies can start tackling negative emissions today and what it will take to build a fair, safe, and affordable market for these new negative emission technologies.

To stick with our race to net zero analogy: The first part is about setting the right goals and mapping out your path to net zero. Crucial in this context: no shortcuts, as these often lead to a dead end. The second part focuses on the essential tools and resources you'll need for this race. Just as a running watch and proper shoes are vital for a marathon, the different carbon removal methods are key on your journey to net zero. We'll show you how negative emission technologies can play a pivotal role in this race. And in the final part, we discuss how you can start running today – no more waiting on the sidelines.

We didn't want to write a dry textbook, so we intentionally avoided bogging down the text with too much academic detail. However, for those interested in the details, you'll find all the relevant sources listed at the end of the book. What's particularly important to us is that you come away from each chapter with clear, actionable steps. To help with this, each chapter begins with an overview of the content and ends with a summary section titled "For those in a hurry." The book is designed to be modular, so you can jump right into the chapters that interest you the most.

We want to reiterate that we strongly believe that negative emission approaches can play a critical role in helping companies and countries achieve zero emissions. This includes everything from nature-based solutions, such as the regeneration of tropical ecosystems, to high-tech methods that resemble giant CO_2 vacuum cleaners. However, at the corporate level, the top priority must always be to reduce your emissions first.

Of course, technology isn't the whole solution; tackling the climate crisis requires more than just new technologies. But these innovations are central to the effort – just as solar and wind power have already become indispensable in the fight against climate change.

You may have noticed that we use the term "climate neutrality" instead of "net zero" on the cover. As we'll explain in Chapter 2, these terms are not synonymous. So why did we choose "climate neutrality"? In short, while "net zero" is technically more accurate, it's not a term that most readers are familiar with. We chose "climate neutrality" because it resonates more broadly, but when we say it, we mean net zero.

So, let's get on our marks – and ready, set, go!

Ben & Marian

PART I
THE RACE TO NET ZERO
WHERE ARE WE NOW AND WHERE DO WE NEED TO GO?

CHAPTER 1
THE PATH TO NET ZERO

> "It ain't what you don't know that gets you into trouble.
> It's what you know for sure that just ain't so."
>
> Attributed to Mark Twain, origin unknown

The history of many companies can be encapsulated in a single, sobering sentence: If you don't recognize the signs of the times, you're destined for extinction. This is precisely what happened to Blockbuster.

Blockbuster's rapid ascent to becoming one of the largest video rental giants in the U.S. began in the 1980s. At its peak, the blue and yellow "Blockbuster" sign, which resembled a torn-off movie ticket, was displayed on more than 9,000 stores nationwide.

But despite its meteoric rise, trouble was brewing beneath the surface. Many customers were becoming increasingly frustrated with the hefty late fees for overdue returns. Among these disgruntled customers was Reed Hastings, who balked at paying a 40 USD fine for returning a movie late.

The name Reed Hastings may not be familiar to everyone, but the company he founded certainly is: Netflix. However, Blockbuster's future could have unfolded very differently.

When the founders of Netflix climbed to the 23rd floor of a gleaming steel-and-glass skyscraper, they had one goal in mind: to sell their fledgling company to Blockbuster. They had waited weeks for this meeting, but they couldn't shake their unease.

As Netflix co-founder Marc Randolph later told *Vanity Fair*: "I was already feeling a little like a country mouse in the big city." Blockbuster CEO John Antioco and his legal advisor strode in, dressed in crisp white shirts and polished Italian shoes, while the Netflix team sat in their casual Hawaiian shirts.

At the time, Netflix wasn't in a strong negotiating position. The dot-com bubble had just burst, leaving many investors to pick up the pieces at the dawn of the new millennium.

Blockbuster, with its extensive network of physical stores, seemed like a solid, tangible business. But the Netflix team had done its homework. Reed Hastings leaned forward and delivered what Randolph would later describe as the "shit sandwich" – start with something positive, follow with something negative, then end on a high note.

Yes, Blockbuster had many stores and millions of active customers, but its online business was lagging. So, Hastings proposed a partnership: Netflix would handle the online side of things, while Blockbuster would continue to dominate retail. Hastings sat back, leaving the offer up in the air. Would the CEO take the bait?

"If we were to buy you, what [price] are you thinking?" the Blockbuster CEO asked. A brief silence followed. "50 million," Hastings replied. The CEO, an industry veteran with a calm and approachable demeanor, maintained eye contact with Hastings. Then, something unexpected happened. Slowly, almost imperceptibly, the corners of his mouth began to twitch upward. As Randolph later wrote, "But as soon as I saw it, I knew what was happening: John Antioco was trying not to laugh."

The meeting went downhill after that. The Netflix founders soon found themselves back outside the skyscraper. "Blockbuster doesn't want us," Randolph said with a grim smile. "So now it's clear what we have to do. It looks like we're going to have to kick their ass."

And that's exactly what they did. Today, only one of Blockbuster's 9,000 stores remains. It's in the small town of Bend, Oregon, kept alive by a few thousand loyal fans and curious vacationers. Airbnb has even listed the location where you can spend a nostalgic night.

The fall of Blockbuster was also captured in a documentary film, *The Last Blockbuster*. And fittingly, you can stream it for free – on Netflix.

But Blockbuster wasn't alone in its demise. Many companies fail to recognize or take seriously major external changes that have the potential to disrupt their business. This is especially true for companies that are currently thriving in the existing system; for them, changing course can be particularly challenging. Instead of pivoting to new products or business models, they often focus on refining their existing offerings for their current customer base.

Digitization, as seen in the case of Blockbuster, is one such external change, but other forces like artificial intelligence and demographic shifts also have the potential to be major disruptors. Meanwhile, the average tenure of a company in the U.S. benchmark index has plummeted from 61 years in 1958 to just 18 years today.

But there's another major disruptor looming on the horizon: climate change. People increasingly want to know how companies are managing their environmental footprint. Public criticism is growing, investors are scrutinizing more closely, and political decisions and regulations are tightening. In addition, the resources on which companies depend are becoming scarcer and more expensive – think of rare earths from China or lithium from Chile.

Transitioning to more climate-friendly business practices doesn't necessarily come cheap. But the cost of inaction is even higher. Sooner or later, regulation and competition will force companies to adopt a more sustainable approach. Compared to other megatrends like AI, the upside with climate change is that we have a clear, evidence-based roadmap for the coming decades. While this clarity underscores the gravity of the situation – we're heading for disaster with our eyes wide open – it also means there's still time to change course.

Blockbuster also recognized that digital could become a serious threat. Unfortunately, by the time they acted, it was too late – the ship had sailed.

So, how do we prepare for the world of tomorrow?

> **In this chapter, we'll explore:**
>
> - why ambitious climate targets are critical for preparing for the future,
> - what constitutes an ambitious climate target,
> - why reducing carbon emissions is vital, and why neutralizing any remaining emissions should already be part of your climate strategy today.

The World of Tomorrow

Let's kick things off with a quiz: Which was the most valuable car company in the world in 2023? Volkswagen, Mercedes-Benz, or General Motors? If you guessed one of those, you'd be wrong. As many of you probably know, the answer is Tesla, the electric car maker.

Over the years, established companies have repeatedly misread the writing on the wall, often with near-fatal consequences. Take German energy giant RWE, for example. As recently as 2012, RWE CEO Jürgen Großmann famously claimed that solar energy in Germany made about as much sense as "growing pineapples in Alaska."

In the years that followed, RWE continued to lose ground in the energy transition and increasingly struggled financially. It wasn't until the company shifted its focus to renewable energy that it began to recover. While RWE is still not a perfect example of a green transformation, in recent years, it has become one of the world's largest producers of renewable energy.

There are, of course, many reasons why companies miss out on major trends, including bureaucracy, competition, and poor planning. But this doesn't just happen to careless companies – it also happens to many vigilant companies that invest heavily in new technologies and stay close to their customers.

In areas like artificial intelligence, predicting the pace of technological change and its impact on various industries is incredibly challenging. While some, including those close to Elon Musk, have called for a pause in AI development, many experts believe these concerns may be overly pessimistic.

Climate change, however, presents a different scenario. There is an overwhelming scientific consensus on the risks it poses, and there are well-defined roadmaps on how to halt the rise in global temperatures. These plans are codified in the 2015 Paris Climate Agreement, in which nearly 200 countries pledged to limit global temperature increases to well below 2 degrees Celsius (3.6 degrees Fahrenheit) above pre-industrial levels.

Based on these global commitments, individual countries and regions have developed their own strategies for reducing greenhouse gas emissions and actively removing them from the atmosphere. These strategies show that we are on the verge of significant industrial and political transformations in the coming years.

The European Union has set a target of achieving net zero by 2050, with Germany aiming to reach that goal even earlier, by 2045. By 2030, the EU plans to cut carbon emissions by more than half from 1990 levels, and by 2035, no new combustion engine vehicles will be allowed on the road. Just a few years ago, such ambitious targets would have seemed unthinkable.

But it's not just the EU – the whole world is in a state of flux as the pressure to act mounts. The UK recognized the importance of decisive climate action early on and was among the first major economies to legally commit to achieving net zero by 2050.

Across the pond, the U. S. is aiming for net zero by 2050 as well. Through legislation such as the Inflation Reduction Act, the Biden administration committed significant funding to accelerate the green transition of the world's second-largest emitting economy, though recent political changes might be a temporary setback.

China and India, the world's biggest emerging economies, have both made significant commitments to tackle climate change. China, the largest carbon emitter globally, has pledged to achieve net zero by 2060, aiming to peak carbon emissions before 2030, and India has set a target of reaching net zero by 2070. While still at different stages of development than Western nations, both countries face the challenge of balancing multiple priorities, which adds complexity to the task of aligning decarbonization efforts.

We stand on the threshold of the next industrial revolution. This revolution won't just involve a few "green" companies; it will require a reorientation of the entire economy, from cement, steel, and chemical manufacturers to shipping and aviation. This industrial transformation will touch every aspect of our lives, affecting how we live, what we eat, and how we travel.

Of course, in many areas, progress on climate protection is slower than what is needed to meet these targets. But looking back over the past few years, we can see that policy changes often happen faster than we expect. Sometimes all it takes is a 16-year-old girl in a yellow raincoat holding a sign that says "School strike for climate" to spark massive political shifts.

While progress may not always be linear, the overall direction of travel is clear. For companies, this means that a forward-looking climate strategy should align with the roadmaps set by governments. Specifically, this translates to achieving net zero greenhouse gas emissions by around 2050.

Net Zero?

The concept of net zero can be quite complex – like much in the realm of climate science. We'll try to demystify it for you with an analogy:

Think of the atmosphere as a large bathtub with a faucet and a drain. Now, picture this: Instead of enjoying a relaxing bath with scented candles and herbal additives, you're standing on the edge of the bathtub in a bit of a panic. The faucet is stuck, and water is gushing in. There's a drain, but it's mostly clogged, so the water keeps rising toward the edge of the tub.

You have two options to prevent the water from flooding your entire bathroom. First, you can try to turn off the faucet as much as possible. Second, you can work on unclogging the drain to allow the water to flow out more freely. Clearly, the first priority is to deal with the faucet – if you don't stop the flow, you're in serious trouble.

While wondering whether your insurance will cover water damage, you pull the faucet lever. It moves, but not all the way, and the water continues to rise. In desperation, you reach into the water and begin to unclog the drain. A small whirlpool forms, and some water finally starts to drain away. The drain isn't completely clear, but at least the water is now flowing out again.

At this point, water is still trickling into the tub, but an equal amount is now draining out. The water level stabilizes just below the rim.

In climate terms, this is what we call the equilibrium between emission sources (represented by the tap) and sinks (represented by the drain). The atmosphere stops warming up when we reach this balance – the equivalent of the water level stabilizing in the bathtub. However, because CO_2 is a long-lived gas, we'll have to contend with the effects of the warming already created – like storms, droughts, and other extreme weather events – for the foreseeable future.

As the water in our bathtub analogy stabilizes, so does the global temperature. But there's a way to reduce temperatures, which might be higher than optimal: by continuing to unclog the drain, allowing more water to flow out than is coming in.

Now, if you're a climate expert, you might be thinking about other greenhouse gases, like methane, that are more short-lived than CO_2. But let's keep our example straightforward for now.

So, how do we know how much water we can add to the bathtub before it overflows? Scientists have calculated a "carbon budget" that tells us how much CO_2 we can still emit before we exceed the temperature targets set by the Paris Climate Agreement. Since CO_2 is evenly distributed in the atmosphere, this budget applies globally, to all countries.

This means we know how much time we have left before the water – our planet's temperature – rises too high. But how that budget is distributed among countries, sectors, and individual companies is a more complex question. The Intergovernmental Panel on Climate Change has reviewed more than 200 scenarios that could meet the temperature goals. However, the carbon budget doesn't tell us what a fair allocation would look like across countries, sectors, or companies. We'll explore more on that shortly.

Net zero means that we close the faucet as much as possible, allowing the drain to carry enough water out of the bathtub to prevent flooding. In other words, the water level stabilizes and stops rising. In the context of climate change, achieving net zero means that we've reduced emissions to the point where the amount of greenhouse gases we emit is equal to the amount we remove, so that global temperatures stop rising.

What Makes an Ambitious Climate Target?

In our bathtub analogy, it seems simple enough – just push the lever, and the water flow decreases. But in reality, it's much more complicated. Researchers, policymakers, activists, entrepreneurs, and many others have been trying to reduce the flow for decades, yet more water keeps pouring into the bathtub, and the drain keeps clogging. The result? The bathtub is filling up faster than ever.

This puts us in a race against time. Every year, we get closer to the brink of overflowing. So, the question is: How fast do we need to move, and how can companies adapt to this urgent climate reality?

Like any race, the first step is to define the finish line – where do we want to go? There are plenty of climate targets out there, but many aren't worth the paper they're written on. According to the Net Zero Tracker, two out of three corporate targets don't even meet minimum quality standards, such as setting clear milestones and transparently reporting progress toward net zero.

But one approach stands out for attempting to follow the latest scientific evidence. This evidence-based approach is embodied in the Science Based Targets initiative (SBTi).

Founded in 2015 by a consortium of leading organizations at the intersection of business and the environment, SBTi helps companies align their goals with the Paris Climate Agreement. "SBTi has now become the standard," says independent climate expert Robert Höglund. "There is no real competition."

SBTi helps companies set their own net zero targets that align with scientific climate goals. If your company already has SBTi-approved targets, you can skip to the next chapter. But for everyone else, here's how SBTi works.

First, a company expresses interest in setting science-based targets. The company then develops emission reduction targets based on SBTi's criteria (more on this shortly). These targets are submitted to SBTi for validation, where they are assessed to ensure they meet the required standards. Once validated, these targets are published on the SBTi website, and companies typically make their emissions data public, allowing for annual comparisons against their targets.

But how are these targets defined? SBTi begins by considering the remaining global carbon budget – essentially, the amount of water that can still be poured into the bathtub before it overflows. It then divides that budget over the remaining years to 2050, using a scenario that outlines how much each company must reduce its emissions each year to stay within that limit.

For example, let's take a look at the first company to have its target certified under the SBTi Net-Zero Standard: TDC NET, a Danish company providing digital infrastructure. TDC NET aims to be net zero by 2030 – a very ambitious goal.

Their first priority is to reduce their own emissions. "To us, the best energy is the energy saved," says Peter Søndergaard Andersen, Head of Sustainability at TDC NET, in an interview with SBTi. "Therefore, we invest in the most energy-efficient technologies and work continuously to reduce our network energy consumption by decommissioning legacy technology." These reductions are classified as Scope 1 emissions, which are the direct emissions from a company's operations.

Beyond reducing direct emissions, TDC NET also focuses on the energy it purchases, known as Scope 2 emissions. "To take responsibility for adding renewable energy to the Danish grid," Andersen explains, "TDC NET signed a power purchase agreement in 2021 for four new solar parks in Denmark." By 2028, the company plans to source all its electricity from renewable sources.

Like many companies, TDC NET also faces the challenge of addressing emissions along its value chain, known as Scope 3 emissions. "Our biggest challenge in terms of decarbonization is our value chain emissions, as we have more than 3,500 suppliers worldwide," says Andersen. SBTi requires companies whose Scope 3 emissions account for at least 40 percent of their total emissions to set a target for these emissions as well.

That's why TDC NET launched a program in 2021 to encourage its suppliers to set more ambitious climate targets. They categorized their suppliers into those with high emissions and those with low emissions. The high emitters received support in "setting their own science-based targets with the SBTi," explains Andersen. "We will then move on to the low emitters."

Andersen acknowledges that the net zero target is a complex challenge. However, despite the significant effort involved, he sees positive outcomes. Thanks to its ambitious strategy, TDC NET has been able to raise fresh capital through green bonds. Additionally, the strategy has had a positive impact on employee motivation. "Our colleagues are proud of our contributions," says Andersen.

The Race to Zero with SBTi

TDC NET has set a particularly ambitious target, aiming for net zero by 2030. Most companies that have adopted SBTi targets aim to achieve net zero between 2040 and 2050. The path to net zero is detailed in *The Corporate Net-Zero Standard*, first published in 2021 and updated several times since.

The Net-Zero Standard can be broken down into four key elements:

- a short-term goal (five to ten years),
- a long-term goal (by 2050 or sooner),
- neutralizing emissions through durable carbon removal,
- mitigation efforts outside the value chain.

The first step is to set a short-term goal that can be achieved within the next five to ten years. For Scope 1 and 2 emissions, this means an absolute reduction of at least 4.2 percent per year, while for Scope 3 emissions, a reduction of 2.5 percent is required. For example, a company starting in 2021 would need to cut its Scope 1 and 2 emissions by about half by 2030.

The long-term goal focuses on reaching net zero by 2050 at the latest, with SBTi requiring a reduction of at least 90 percent. However, certain industries, such as power generation and shipping, have stricter deadlines and must achieve this goal by 2040. This is because sectors like green electricity are fundamental to the success of the broader energy transition, which impacts everything from electric mobility to green hydrogen. Without sufficient green electricity, the energy transition cannot succeed.

SBTi also allows companies to set targets based on CO_2 intensity rather than absolute targets, which can be particularly useful for companies in the forestry or agricultural sectors, as well as those experiencing rapid growth. For a company like Tesla, which is expanding rapidly, an absolute reduction in emissions may not be feasible in the short term. However, reducing the CO_2 footprint of each car by using greener components is a more realistic and impactful goal.

SBTi emphasizes the need to significantly reduce a company's own emissions. For most companies, this means achieving at least a 90 percent reduction by 2050, with a substantial portion of this reduction by 2030.

However, SBTi also recognizes that not all emissions can be eliminated. That's why the remaining 10 percent of emissions can be offset through so-called "durable carbon removal." These approaches, which we'll explore in later chapters, involve technologies that remove carbon directly from the air and ensure that it is stored for the long term. Only by using these methods can a company truly achieve net zero. The SBTi reduction pathway is illustrated in the following chart.

Finally, there is the concept of "beyond value chain mitigation." This involves protecting critical carbon sinks, such as tropical rainforests or peatlands, which have significant potential for reducing emissions. However, these efforts do not count toward a company's own emission reduction targets.

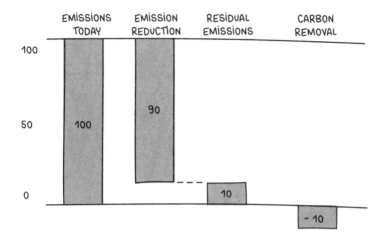

Why distinguish between carbon removal and beyond value chain mitigation? The distinction is rooted in the scientific understanding of net zero. A ton of CO_2 left in the atmosphere will contribute to global warming for thousands of years. To neutralize this impact, carbon must be durably removed from the atmosphere and stored in a way that prevents it from re-entering the atmosphere for an equivalent period of time. This is something that forest conservation projects, for instance, cannot guarantee – if a forest burns down after ten years, the CO_2 stored in those trees will be released back into the atmosphere. In such a scenario, the net zero target is undermined, and the climate continues to warm.

Or, to return to our bathtub analogy, once the water is drained, we have to make sure it doesn't go back into the bathtub.

SBTi is Not Perfect

While SBTi has become the industry standard for setting climate targets, it's important to recognize that the framework is not without its flaws and is still evolving.

One of the main criticisms comes from small and medium-sized businesses. SBTi is often seen as more appropriate for large companies with steady, manageable growth. For companies with fewer than 500 employees, SBTi currently offers only one path: an absolute reduction in their emissions. However, for fast-growing startups, intensity-based targets are often more practical, as absolute reductions in emissions can be nearly impossible in the short term.

Another area where SBTi has historically fallen short is in providing incentives for companies to engage in carbon removal already today. Under the guidelines at the time of writing in October 2024, companies with net zero targets are only required to neutralize their remaining emissions by the target date, typically between 2040 and 2050. However, the guidelines will likely change soon. "To meet net zero commitments, companies can't defer carbon removal to the final years," argues climate expert Robert Höglund. "Interim targets, potentially rolling out in the near term, will require businesses to scale their removal activities incrementally, setting clear and achievable benchmarks that align with science-based climate strategies."

Yet, behind all these details, a bigger question is lurking: How realistic are these net zero targets? As British economist Dieter Helm points out, "When it comes to net zero, the easy bit is announcing targets. It's a competitive business: Who can come up with ever more ambitious targets?"

A 2023 analysis by the New Climate Institute found that even under SBTi, many companies fail to provide transparent information on how they plan to meet their targets. This issue is particularly pronounced for Scope 3 emissions, which often constitute the largest share of a company's carbon footprint. SBTi itself acknowledges that only about half of the companies that have adopted science-based targets transparently document their progress toward both short- and long-term goals.

SBTi recently found itself in hot water over its stance on Scope 3 emissions. On April 9, 2024, the organization's CEO made waves by announcing a shift in policy, allowing companies to use carbon credits for their Scope 3 emissions, which sparked a heated debate. Most carbon credits are based on paying someone else to reduce emissions, but as we discuss in Chapter 2, this often doesn't lead to the expected emission reductions. While some saw this as a progressive move, the reaction within SBTi was different.

Many of SBTi's staff and experts penned open letters criticizing the decision. Their concern? The expanded use of carbon credits could lead to corporate greenwashing and would undermine the credibility of the organization. According to the critics, this policy shift seemed to bypass SBTi's usual scientific checks and balances. The scientific teams, who normally play a key role in guiding such decisions, weren't even consulted beforehand.

In the wake of this internal backlash, the SBTi Board of Trustees quickly issued a clarification stating that no actual changes had been made to the organization's current standards. The Board emphasized that any future changes regarding the use of carbon credits for Scope 3 emissions would be based on scientific evidence and would follow a rigorous process, including research, public consultation, and technical review.

Still, the controversy didn't just fizzle out, culminating in the resignation of SBTi's CEO in early July 2024. As a response to the ongoing uproar, SBTi committed to publishing a discussion paper outlining potential updates to their Scope 3 guidelines. The goal? To initiate a transparent, evidence-based process for any future revisions, making sure science stays at the heart of their standards.

Despite its imperfections, SBTi remains the best available framework for companies committed to reducing their carbon footprint.

While the guidelines will evolve over time, they already provide a clear, science-based direction for businesses.

Why Some U. S. Companies Are Still Struggling with SBTi

Since its launch in 2015, SBTi has gained significant traction. As of August 2024, over 5,800 companies had set science based targets, with another 2,700 in the process of validating their targets. Collectively, these companies represent about one-third of global market capitalization. In contrast to the global doubling of the companies with science-based targets in 2023, the U. S. share of large companies committed to SBTi in the S&P 500 declined from 42 percent in 2022 to 34 percent in 2023. Major players like Microsoft, Walmart, and P&G are still committed, but other giants such as Amazon have dropped out. Why?

Companies participating in SBTi must develop and submit plans within 24 months of declaring their intent to set science-based targets. Between 2022 and 2023, SBTi temporarily flagged more than 20 U. S. companies and many others around the world for failing to submit their emission reduction plans on time. These developments seem to align with the broader challenges that large U. S. companies face in accurately reporting their emissions. In fact, a study of financial service provider MSCI found that many have fallen behind their international peers in disclosing climate risks. Notably, U. S. regulators have also exempted large firms from the obligation to report Scope 3 emissions for the time being.

Despite a decline in the number of large U. S. firms with science-based targets, the overall number of large companies accredited by SBTi continues to grow significantly.

This growth is likely driven by external pressure from major investors, particularly groups like Climate Action 100+, which are urging lagging companies to take more decisive action. Additionally, increasing global climate reporting requirements continue to drive participation.

At the same time, we are seeing a significant increase in the participation of small and medium-sized companies, which have historically been hesitant to adopt science-based targets due to the personnel and financial costs involved. This shift is largely due to SBTi's efforts to simplify the validation process for smaller organizations, making it more accessible and cost-effective for them to commit to science-based targets.

However, as developing accurate CO_2 monitoring and setting clear targets become essential steps in preparing for future regulations, some companies – both large and small – are unfortunately looking for shortcuts in the race to net zero. Rather than focusing on reducing their emissions and using high-quality carbon removal credits to offset the rest, these organizations are turning to questionable carbon credits. In the next chapter, we'll explore why these shortcuts are problematic and what constitutes a high-quality carbon credit.

For Those in a Hurry

- It's a common assumption that companies fail because of carelessness or poor management.
- However, the reality is often the opposite: Companies excel at selling existing products and services, which can make them blind or inattentive to emerging trends.
- Climate change offers many business opportunities, but it also poses significant risks to established companies and their business models.
- Regulatory changes are often sudden. Setting ambitious climate targets now can help companies prepare for the future.

- There are numerous climate target frameworks for companies, but the Science Based Targets initiative (SBTi) has become the de facto standard, grounded in scientific research.
- SBTi focuses on two main strategies for achieving net zero: reducing a company's own emissions and using durable carbon removal to neutralize residual emissions.
- While actions beyond a company's own value chain, such as supporting forest conservation projects, are important, they cannot be counted toward the company's own emission reductions.
- In the next chapter, we'll explore what durable carbon removal is – and what it isn't.

CHAPTER 2
THE CARBON CREDIT JUNGLE

> "A bad system will beat a good person every time."
>
> W. Edwards Deming, statistician

The crowd at the Boston Marathon was astounded when 26-year-old Rosie Ruiz crossed the finish line. The clock showed two hours and 31 minutes – a record-breaking time for a woman on that course in 1980. First place on the podium, just shy of the world record.

But who was this runner with short, jet-black hair? None of the other elite runners recognized her. Even more puzzling, she didn't know anything about running. When asked about her running pace, she couldn't provide an answer – something even most amateur runners would know.

There was something else odd about her finish: Rosie Ruiz barely seemed to be sweating. Despite supposedly running at full speed for over two hours, her hair was perfectly in place, and her face wasn't flushed, as *The Times* reported. When asked about it, she nonchalantly replied, "I just got up this morning with a lot of energy."

Doubts grew as none of the other runners had seen her on the course. Two men later recalled seeing a woman suddenly sprint onto the track just before the finish line. That woman was Rosie Ruiz. A photographer also remembered seeing her on the subway earlier – she had said she was injured but still wanted to see the finish.

Although Ruiz insisted that she had run the marathon, she was stripped of her medal. She later confessed to a friend that she hadn't actually run the race. He recalled, "She jumped out of the crowd, not knowing that the first woman hadn't gone by yet. Believe me, she was as shocked as anyone when she came in first." Her creative approach to the rules would later land her in jail when she was caught with a stash of cocaine.

What does this story have to do with the race to net zero? In short, there are no shortcuts. And more importantly, the journey ahead will be challenging and exhausting.

Yet, if you walk down a supermarket aisle today, you might get the impression that we're almost there. "Carbon neutral" labels greet you from every direction. Oil companies advertise carbon neutral driving, airlines promote carbon neutral flying, and even a Swiss mountain railway once advertised carbon neutral skiing.

Some companies take their sustainability messaging up another notch. You might spot the label "Climate positive" on baby food in the supermarket. Those Spaghetti Bolognese aren't just good for little tummies – they're supposedly good for the planet, too.

A whiskey distillery in the U.S. goes even further, offering a carbon negative bourbon. It claims to be 1,000 percent negative, purchasing ten times as many carbon credits as it emits, primarily from renewable energy and forestry projects. True to the spirit "drink for the planet."

In recent years, however, there has been growing concern that the voluntary carbon market suffers from significant quality issues. Several studies across different sectors suggest that a large proportion of carbon credits in the voluntary carbon market do not actually reduce emissions.

To be clear, we're not here to single out or criticize any particular company. We recognize that many have attempted to offset their emissions to the best of their knowledge and intentions. The vast majority of carbon credits have also been certified by seemingly trustworthy organizations.

But as we discussed in the last chapter, the Science Based Targets initiative is very clear in its guidance: As a company, your primary focus should be on reducing your own emissions. Only after you've done everything possible to cut emissions should you consider offsetting the rest.

These residual emissions could potentially be offset today through the voluntary carbon market, where a variety of carbon credits are available for purchase. Each credit represents 1 ton of CO_2 that has been avoided, reduced, or removed from the atmosphere.

However, the voluntary carbon market is a complex and often confusing landscape. It's a jungle of different types of carbon credits, multiple players, and varying standards. And as of 2025, the market is in a state of significant uncertainty. Due to growing doubts about the actual environmental impact of carbon credits, the voluntary carbon market experienced its first decline in 2022 after years of growth.

As recently as 2021, consultants of McKinsey & Company predicted that the voluntary credit market could grow 15-fold by 2030. But recently, the market has shrunk significantly. Now, the market is suddenly facing an uncertain future. In this chapter, we'll guide you through the jungle of the voluntary carbon market.

In this chapter, we'll explore:

- how the voluntary carbon market came to be,
- how carbon crediting projects work,
- what is going wrong in the voluntary carbon market,
- what makes a high-quality carbon credit and how it should be integrated into corporate strategies,
- what lessons can be drawn from the challenges facing the current carbon market.

How the Voluntary Carbon Market Came to Be

In 1987, the CEO of the energy company Applied Energy Services (AES) approached Sheryl Sturges with a concern that would soon shape the future of carbon offsetting, as reported by NPR. "Sheryl, I'm concerned that global warming may be a real thing and I'm concerned that AES is contributing to it." AES was building a new coal-fired power plant that would pump enormous amounts of CO_2 into the atmosphere. "Can you find a way to [...] minimize or avoid our emissions in the area?" her boss wanted to know.

At the time, Sheryl Sturges wasn't deeply involved in environmental issues, despite her father being an ecologist. However, her boss's concern piqued her curiosity. She borrowed books from the library to learn about climate change. Even back then, there already was some understanding that CO_2 played a role in global warming, but the strategies for managing carbon emissions were as underdeveloped as the science itself.

"There's a wide range of things you can do with CO_2. You can inject it in soda. It makes soda bubble," Sturges later explained in an interview with NPR. "That is awesome, but it's not very practical. Apparently we don't drink enough Pepsi to use the carbon emissions from a coal plant." Clearly, other ideas were needed.

The concept of liquefying CO_2, storing it in tanks, and sinking it into the ocean was quickly dismissed due to the high cost. Sheryl kept looking for solutions, and one day she came across a scientific study that sparked an idea: Trees absorb CO_2 and store it in their trunks and leaves. "Everybody learns this in school," she said. This led to the novel idea of planting trees to offset the carbon emissions from the coal-fired power plant.

Sturges took her idea to Paul Faeth, who worked at the World Resources Institute (WRI), a prominent environmental research organization. Incidentally, the WRI was one of the founding members of the Science Based Targets initiative, which we discussed in the previous chapter.

WRI's experts confirmed that planting trees could indeed help offset the plant's emissions. At first, Sturges envisioned planting a small forest near the plant to absorb the CO_2. But when the researchers ran the numbers, it was clear that wouldn't be feasible: She'd need 52 million trees, far more than the plant's site could accommodate.

"I've got this crazy idea," Sturges recalled saying. "Do I have to plant the trees in Connecticut or could they be anywhere?" Faeth assured her that the trees could be planted anywhere, as it did not matter where the CO_2 was removed from the atmosphere. Soon they were planting trees in the mountains of Guatemala, marking the birth of the world's first carbon crediting project.

Carbon credits that are used to "offset" emissions are mechanisms that balance emissions in one location by avoiding, reducing, or removing emissions elsewhere. In this case, the CO_2 emissions from a coal-fired power plant in the U. S. were offset by a reforestation project in Central America. Typically, such carbon credits are certified by a government or independent organization. These credits – usually representing 1 ton of CO_2 – can then be used by a company for its own offsetting purposes, as AES has done, or sold to others.

Major newspapers quickly picked up on the story. In 1988, *TIME* magazine ran a headline that read "Antidote for a Smokestack," highlighting the innovative approach to addressing carbon emissions. Suddenly, a wide variety of companies wanted to get involved. Car rental companies, airlines, and major banks like HSBC all expressed interest in planting trees to offset their emissions. Sturges' project fundamentally changed how the world looked at CO_2.

No longer was CO_2 just a gas that contributed to global warming. "We were trying to commoditize carbon so that you could trade it." Carbon had become a commodity, much like coffee or corn, that could be traded on a global scale. For the first time, a ton of CO_2 that wasn't emitted had a monetary value – just a few cents per ton for AES. This non-emitted ton could be sold as a carbon credit.

From these humble beginnings, the voluntary carbon market has grown into a billion-dollar industry. By 2022, the market was valued at around 2 billion USD. Afforestation and forest protection projects are still among the most common types of carbon credits today, but the market has expanded to include renewable energy projects, efficient cookstoves, waste gas abatement, and more.

Carbon project developers – which includes private firms, NGOs, and government agencies – received a significant government boost in the 2000s with the launch of the United Nations Clean Development Mechanism. It allowed countries with reduction targets under the Kyoto Protocol – the precursor to the Paris Climate Agreement – to finance climate projects in other countries. Thousands of projects were registered, resulting in the issuance of more than 1 billion tons of carbon credits.

But even in those early days, doubts began to surface about the actual emission reductions claimed by these projects. Experts questioned the effectiveness of the scheme, while environmental activists criticized the approach as a modern form of selling indulgences, where money could seemingly buy absolution for environmental sins. As *The New Yorker* reported, the first project that AES developed in Guatemala fell far short of expectations, achieving only about 10 percent of the expected emission reductions.

In addition, the approach was taken to the point of absurdity when first websites appeared, asking unfaithful spouses to offset their infidelity: "By paying Cheat Neutral, you're funding monogamy-boosting offset projects."

How Carbon Crediting Projects Work

To understand why early doubts arose about the environmental impact of these projects, it's important to look at how crediting projects are developed.

Unlike Sheryl Sturges' original afforestation project with Applied Energy Services, most of today's carbon credits are based on avoiding emissions that would otherwise have occurred. Instead of creating new forests through afforestation, many projects focus on protecting existing forests that are at risk of being cut down.

Let's explore how such a project is developed by examining the Kariba forest conservation project in Zimbabwe, which has received considerable media attention. The credits from this project were sold by South Pole, the world's largest vendor of carbon credits.

According to *The New Yorker*, the project began with an email from Zimbabwean businessman Steve Wentzel. Wentzel had no prior experience in the voluntary carbon market; he made his money from financial dealings in the tax havens of Guernsey and Mauritius.

He came into possession of a piece of forest in Zimbabwe because a business partner was unable to repay his debts. Initially, Wentzel saw no value in the land until he discovered carbon credits while browsing Google. "Let's see whether we can recoup our money that way," he told *The New Yorker*.

How should the forest be protected? Together with South Pole, Wentzel developed a strategy. The forest was being cleared by local farmers to make room for their cattle and crops. The idea was to provide the local population with alternative, sustainable sources of income. For instance, they proposed training the locals in beekeeping, which would allow them to sell honey without cutting down the forest. The avoided deforestation could then be monetized as carbon credits.

To promote the benefits of forest conservation to the local community, leaflets were distributed, featuring an illustration of dollar signs growing on trees. Wentzel was so persuasive that he managed to expand his lands to an area of 810,000 hectares (2 million acres), equivalent to 1.5 million American football fields.

Wentzel promised the local people that they would get the lion's share of the project's revenue – and that they wouldn't have to do anything in return. "We didn't ask them to get up in the morning, we didn't ask them to do push-ups, we didn't ask the birds to fly backwards. It was just a net positive for them," Wentzel told *The New Yorker*.

Wentzel founded a company, Carbon Green Investments, which he registered in the tax haven of Guernsey. Soon after, he had grown to become one of the largest developers of carbon crediting projects in the world.

However, in order to sell credits from the forest conservation project, it was necessary to estimate how many emissions would actually be saved. In the absence of a government organization to regulate the voluntary carbon market, Verra, an American NGO, stepped in to fill the gap. Since then, Verra has been setting the rules under which such projects can sell carbon credits. Today, Verra certifies about two-thirds of the voluntary carbon market, with about half of those credits coming from forest conservation projects like Kariba, according to *The New Yorker*.

To register the Kariba forest conservation project, South Pole had to calculate how many carbon credits could be issued over 30 years under Verra's rules. This required estimating what would happen if the project didn't exist.

To make this estimation, they had to create a "counterfactual scenario" – a kind of alternate reality that asked: What would happen if the forest wasn't protected by the project? To answer this question, they used a reference region, selecting nearby forest areas that were similar to the Kariba project but not protected. In these areas, for example, local farmers wouldn't receive training in beekeeping. However, these areas had common characteristics, such as a similar population density.

Using Verra's methodology, they applied historical deforestation trends to the Kariba project area to construct this alternative reality. The result was striking: The projection showed that almost the entire project area would be deforested over the 30-year period. Based on this, the project developer estimated that nearly 200 million carbon credits could be issued.

These credits were then sold to companies such as Volkswagen, Gucci, and Nestlé through South Pole. For example, Nestlé's claim that KitKat is carbon neutral was based on credits from the Kariba project.

What Is Going Wrong in the Voluntary Carbon Market?

But doubts about the Kariba project's true environmental impacts are growing. The first cracks appeared when forestry expert Elias Ayrey shared a satellite image of the Kariba project on LinkedIn. "I just reviewed a #carbon project that's likely receiving more than 30x as many credits as it should," the expert wrote. He works for Renoster, an independent carbon credit analysis company.

The reference region showed significantly less deforestation than the project developers had assumed, meaning the project's avoided deforestation was much less than expected. Ayrey didn't mince words, ending his post with, "All opinions are my own. And my own opinion is that everyone involved with this project should be arrested."

Verra has plans for such contingencies: Every ten years, the original estimates would be reviewed. If it turns out that too many carbon credits have been issued, the next phase of the project won't issue any new credits until the surplus has been recouped. However, given the low rate of deforestation in the surrounding regions, experts doubt that the project can protect enough forest to actually offset the excess credits already issued.

Verra has also taken precautions against such situations in the form of an insurance policy: A portion of the credits issued is placed in a pot called "the buffer pool," where credits from various projects are held back. If a project falls short of expectations, Verra can draw on these.

The problem? The quality issues surrounding the Kariba forest conservation project aren't an isolated case. Many of the other carbon credits in this insurance pool potentially don't represent actual reductions either. In fact, a study published in the prestigious journal *Science* found that 26 projects certified by Verra achieved less than 10 percent of their estimated emission reductions. That number is just staggering. It's like signing up for a marathon and only running the first two miles.

And it's not just forestry projects where quality concerns crop up. Take, for example, a wind energy project in Turkey designed to replace coal-fired electricity and cut carbon emissions. The developer can sell both electricity and credits for avoided emissions. Now, if those carbon credits were what made the project profitable, then those carbon credits could be sold.

However, several studies have shown that many renewable energy projects that were supposed to be financed by the sale of carbon credits were just as financially attractive as those that didn't involve selling credits, regardless of whether they later sold credits or not. When this happens, the principle of "additionality" isn't met. Additionality means that only the sale of carbon credits makes a project financially viable. Additionality answers the simple question: Would the mitigation activity have occurred without the revenue from the sale of carbon credits? If the project would have happened anyway, it is not additional.

Doubts are also emerging about the effectiveness of cookstove projects. These stoves are used in low- and middle-income countries to replace traditional cooking methods that are not energy efficient and lead to emissions. The idea is similar to forest protection or renewable energy projects: If a more efficient stove is used, the avoided emissions can be sold as credits. However, a study by the University of Berkeley estimates that these projects have sold many more credits than they have actually saved in CO_2.

Ben led an international team of scientists to systematically assess how much of the claimed emission reductions had been achieved according to the latest science across all the major carbon crediting project types. Our team analyzed almost 1 billion tons of carbon credits, and found that less than 16 percent of the issued credits across six major project categories constituted real emission reductions. Hence, the above-mentioned challenges in the voluntary carbon market are not just single projects; they are ultimately systematic failures of the market

In addition to ensuring that projects genuinely reduce emissions, climate credits must also guarantee the durability of carbon reduction. As you may recall from Chapter 1, it's crucial that carbon reductions or removals last as long as CO_2 remains in the atmosphere – meaning thousands of years. Short-term forest protection projects simply can't meet this requirement, which is a key reason why the Science Based Targets initiative generally does not allow companies to count such short-term emission reductions toward their net zero targets.

Moreover, it's vital that crediting projects don't come at the expense of local communities. There have been cases of local farmers being displaced to make way for reforestation projects. A recent inquiry by *The Guardian* and the Dutch investigative portal *Follow The Money* even suggested that a Chinese biogas project selling carbon credits may have benefited from the forced labor of the Muslim Uyghur minority.

But rather than focusing solely on individual market players like South Pole, it's important to take a step back and look at the bigger picture. The most fundamental problem with the current market is systemic.

Neither the project developer nor Verra has an incentive to issue credits conservatively. For example, Verra receives a few cents for each credit it puts on the market. While this doesn't necessarily mean Verra has issued too many credits, the conflict of interest is clear. Credit sellers also have an incentive to issue as many credits as possible, since they profit from each one.

Amid these challenges, many voices are increasingly questioning the legitimacy of the entire market. For example, climate expert Danny Cullenward lamented in *The New Yorker*: "There are a lot of us who believe that this resembles an elaborate fraud." However, not all carbon credits are hot air. There are different species in the CO_2 jungle, and some are essential on the path to net zero.

Different Types of Credits

The problems with the current market and SBTi's clear guidance signal that we're on the verge of a significant shift in the voluntary carbon market.

In short, we need to move from a system that has largely relied on avoiding emissions through forest protection and short-term carbon removal projects, such as afforestation, to one that emphasizes long-term carbon removal. To understand this, let's take a quick look at the different types of credits.

Broadly speaking, carbon credits fall into two main categories: those based on carbon avoidance and reduction, and those focused on carbon removal. Carbon avoidance and reduction is the dominant sector in the current market. Credits can be further subdivided based on the type and duration of carbon storage.

This breakdown leads to five sub-categories, which are illustrated in the accompanying diagram with examples of each project type.

These categories are drawn from the Oxford Principles for Net Zero Aligned Carbon Offsetting.

TYPE	AVOIDANCE/REDUCTION			REMOVAL	
STORAGE	NO STORAGE	SHORT-TERM	LONG-TERM	SHORT-TERM	LONG-TERM
METHOD	RENEWABLE ENERGIES	AVOIDED DEFORESTATION	CCS	AFFORESTATION	DACCS

The first group of carbon crediting projects typically focuses on avoiding CO_2 emissions. Take the aforementioned wind turbine, for example. By increasing the amount of green electricity fed into the grid, this type of project can reduce the need for coal-fired power plants to generate electricity, thereby avoiding CO_2 emissions.

Another important subset involves reducing emissions from existing carbon sinks that store CO_2 in the short term (Group 2). These include forest conservation projects aimed at reducing deforestation. By preventing deforestation, these projects ensure that the carbon already stored in forests remains in place.

Group 3 includes carbon crediting projects that avoid carbon and store it for the long term. These are primarily Carbon Capture and Storage (CCS) projects, which capture CO_2 from industrial plants or power plants at the smokestack and store it underground for the long term (we'll discuss this in more detail when we look at carbon removal methods in Chapter 6). However, these projects currently play a negligible role in the market.

Group 4 covers projects that remove carbon from the air and store it in the short term. These include afforestation projects, initiatives to enhance soil carbon content, and the restoration of damaged ecosystems, which we discuss in Chapter 4.

The last group is a central focus of this book, but it is currently almost non-existent in the market: carbon removal projects with long-term storage. According to SBTi, this is the only group that can be used to credibly offset residual emissions. Chapters 5 and 6 delve deeper into these project categories.

So, while there is a range of carbon credits available, according to SBTi, the vast majority are unsuitable for achieving net zero. This doesn't mean that protecting forests, expanding renewable energy, or providing energy-efficient cookstoves to low-income households aren't important – they absolutely are. But the goal of net zero can only be achieved through durable carbon removal.

Carbon Credits for Net Zero

So, what sets apart high-quality removal credits that really get us to net zero?

High-quality carbon removal credits have a few characteristics. In a nutshell, these credits are based on carbon removal that wouldn't have happened without the funding from carbon credits. It should also be durable and can be accurately measured and monitored. These solutions should be scalable without significant neg-

 ADDITIONAL CARBON REMOVAL

 DURABILITY

 MONITORING, REPORTING, AND VERIFICATION (MRV)

 SIDE EFFECTS

 SCALABILITY

ative side effects. We'll illustrate this with the example of direct air carbon capture and storage (DACCS). DACCS involves removing CO_2 directly from the air and storing it in geological repositories – more on this in Chapter 6.

Unlike forest conservation projects, which aim to prevent the release of carbon that's already been absorbed, carbon removal projects involve removing CO_2 directly from the air. In the case of DACCS, CO_2 is directly filtered from the ambient air through chemical processes, while the remaining air is safely released back into the atmosphere.

Second, this carbon removal is stored long-term. This is what sets DACCS apart from afforestation projects, which also remove carbon from the air but do not store it long-term. When a forest burns down, the stored CO_2 is released back into the atmosphere. To truly offset CO_2 emissions that will remain in the atmosphere for thousands of years, carbon crediting projects must ensure that the carbon is removed for a similarly long period of time. This is what we call durability. For example, carbon captured by DACCS plants in Iceland is stored deep underground, where it turns to stone over time.

Third, it's critical to ensure that this durable removal is properly measured and monitored – this is called "Monitoring, Reporting, and Verification" (MRV). We need to learn from the pitfalls of the old carbon market and avoid conflicts of interest, such as ensuring that the payment of the certifier is independent of the issuance of the offset credits, or that external auditors aren't paid by the project developers themselves. In DACCS, sensors can be used to verify that carbon is actually being captured and stored as promised.

Fourth, we need to ensure that these projects, or any part of their value chain, don't create significant negative side effects. Ideally, high-quality credits should not only avoid contributing to existing climate injustices but should actively help alleviate them. More on this in Chapter 8. For DACCS, this means involving local communities in the planning, construction, and operation processes and monitoring other environmental impacts, such as water use.

Finally, it's clear that we're going to need vast amounts of carbon removal in the future – possibly larger than the emissions of the U.S. today. This makes the scalability of these removal methods critical; we simply don't have the luxury of time for small, incremental approaches.

To Achieve Net Zero, We Need Carbon Removal

But why do we need high-quality credits to get to net zero? Why aren't simple avoidance projects enough? This question brings us to the difference between net zero and climate neutrality, a distinction we'll explore briefly here.

Let's break it down with three simple examples. Suppose Company A emits 1 ton of CO_2, and Company B also emits 1 ton elsewhere. In total, 2 tons of CO_2 are emitted. Now, if Company A pays Company B not to emit 1 ton, Company A can claim to be "climate neutral" because it has offset its emissions. However, the overall situation remains unchanged – 1 ton of CO_2 is still emitted into the atmosphere, so net zero isn't achieved. Only when 1 ton of CO_2 has been removed from the air for every emitted ton of CO_2, do we speak of net zero, as shown in the chart.

It's crucial to remember that for net zero, a ton of carbon must be removed from the air for as long as the emitted ton of CO_2 remains in the atmosphere – ideally, at least 1,000 years. This means that for a company to be truly net zero, it must also remove any remaining emissions from the atmosphere for the same period of time. Simply paying another company not to emit isn't enough to achieve net zero. While there are emissions, such as methane, that remain in

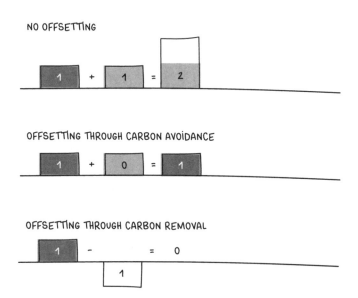

the atmosphere for shorter periods of time, discussing them is beyond the scope of this book.

To tackle climate change, it's not enough to be carbon neutral; net emissions must drop to zero. Think back to the bathtub: The water that continues to flow in must be drained at the same rate through the drain to prevent flooding.

The carbon removal industry needs to move at lightning speed. Countries like the U.S. aim to reach net zero by 2050 – that's just 25 years from now (as of 2025), the blink of an eye in the history of technology. It's a genuine race to net zero.

What does this mean for businesses? We'll dive into that in the next section.

The Way Forward

We hope this brief tour of the current carbon credits landscape has made it clear that the voluntary carbon market alone won't get us to net zero.

When companies claim to be carbon neutral, they often rely on carbon credits. However, as we've discussed in this chapter, there are significant doubts about the effectiveness of these carbon crediting projects. In addition, these projects only avoid carbon emissions in the short term, making them unsuitable for truly "neutralizing" residual emissions.

This doesn't mean that forest conservation and related projects aren't important. Protecting forests is a vital pillar of climate action, with additional benefits like safeguarding biodiversity and supporting the livelihoods of many communities.

However, these projects aren't fit for achieving a net zero target. That's why SBTi clearly states that "The use of carbon credits must not be counted as emission reductions toward the progress of companies' near-term or long-term science-based targets."

The situation is different when it comes to credits from long-term carbon removal projects. These play a central role in a company's path to net zero, as SBTi emphasizes in its guidelines.

But even here, there are various approaches, each with its pros and cons, which we'll explore in the following chapters.

For Those in a Hurry

- The voluntary carbon market has grown into a billion-dollar industry since its beginnings in the 1980s.
- The current market is dominated by credits based on carbon avoidance or reduction.
- However, as the market has grown, so have doubts about the environmental effectiveness of the credits sold.
- Several studies suggest that forest conservation projects have preserved significantly less forest than project developers claim.
- Similar quality issues are being uncovered in other sectors, such as renewable energy projects and efficient cookstove initiatives.

PART II
CARBON REMOVAL
WHICH SOLUTIONS CAN GET US TO THE FINISH LINE?

CHAPTER 3
OVERVIEW OF THE MOST IMPORTANT CARBON REMOVAL METHODS

> "Adopt the pace of nature. Her secret is patience."
>
> Ralph Waldo Emerson, philosopher

33 million – no, we are not talking about tons of carbon dioxide this time, but the number of followers of the YouTube channel *thatlittlepuff* as of October 2024, earning it a place in *The Guinness Book of World Records*.

So far, so unremarkable in a world where more than half a billion people follow the life of soccer star Cristiano Ronaldo on Instagram. What makes it special and the reason for the world record: Puff is a cat – not just any cat, but officially "the most watched cat on YouTube," according to *The Guinness Book*, loved for its outrageous costumes and antics.

But cats have not always been the Internet darlings they are today. In medieval times, they did not exactly win popularity contests compared to more "useful" animals like chickens, pigs, and cattle, which at least provided meat or milk. So, it was not uncommon for cunning merchants to trick buyers into purchasing a cat instead of the suckling pig they had been promised, only for the buyer to discover the deception at home. This gave rise to the saying "let the cat out of the bag."

As we saw in the previous chapter, the voluntary carbon market has had its share of "cats in bags," too. With limited transparency, companies often found themselves purchasing carbon credits, only to discover later that the credits were of poor quality.

At the same time, the reality is clear: Companies will need to offset their unavoidable emissions in the future, ideally with carbon removal credits. But these are fundamentally different from the avoidance credits we have seen before. If evaluating the quality of seemingly straightforward reduction methods – like avoiding deforestation or investing in renewable energy projects – was challenging, the new world of carbon removal presents even steeper hurdles.

And yes, there are still some tricky cats lurking in this new space. While the fundamental principle of carbon removal is different from carbon avoidance, risks of credit integrity or potential negative side effects still exist. As is often the case, knowledge is power. So, over the next three chapters, we'll introduce you to the main carbon removal methods, dive into their pros and cons, and provide practical advice to help you navigate this evolving landscape and make informed decisions.

In this chapter, we'll explore:

- the two distinct carbon cycles,
- which carbon removal methods use which cycle.

One World, Two Cycles

To grasp the various carbon removal methods, it's crucial to first understand the fundamentals of the Earth's carbon cycles. Essentially, there are two: a fast, biological carbon cycle and a slow, geological carbon cycle.

To illustrate, let's take a trip down memory lane to the days before online banking and robo-advisors – back when you knew your bank advisor by name and carried your little passbook to the bank every few months, with home cupboards overflowing with paper bank statements.

Think of your regular checking account as the fast carbon cycle. Your paycheck lands at the start of the month, but expenses quickly eat away at it – rent, groceries, school fees, and that irresistible limited-edition paperback – until you are relieved to see a black zero on your statement by month's end.

The fast carbon cycle operates similarly. CO_2 changes form relatively quickly – plants grow and absorb CO_2 through photosynthesis, then decompose, are consumed, or are burned for generating heat and energy. In every case, CO_2 is released again, directly or indirectly. If there were bank statements for the fast carbon cycle, there would be a lot to read.

On the flip side, the slow carbon cycle is more like an old-fashioned savings account. Not much happens over a long time – savings are occasionally deposited, interest is paid, and in rare cases, money is withdrawn. Otherwise, it's steady as she goes. In the slow carbon cycle, nothing happens for a long time either. CO_2 remains stored for thousands of years, often in rocks, mountains, or fossil fuels like coal, natural gas, and oil. Because of these forms, it's known as the geological cycle.

Without human interference, the Earth's carbon balance would also stay in balance at a black zero. The planet naturally regulates the input and output of carbon – but over millennia, not months. The natural process predominantly responsible for this is called "weathering" and is explored further in Chapter 5. However, human activities – particularly the use of fossil fuels – have tipped the scales, creating a carbon debt. Now, we need to repay that debt by actively removing and storing CO_2.

All current carbon removal methods leverage one or both of

these carbon cycles. The first category of solutions operates within the fast carbon cycle, primarily through nature-based processes like photosynthesis. In this book, we'll explore the following methods: reforestation, regenerative agriculture, peatland restoration, biomass conservation, and blue carbon (CO_2 storage in marine ecosystems). Beyond removing CO_2, these methods offer numerous ecosystem benefits, so much so that these benefits might eventually outweigh the value of carbon removal itself.

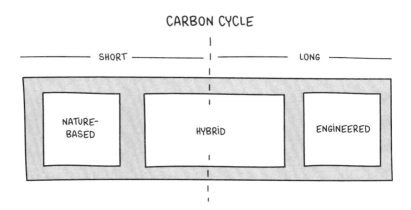

The second category involves methods that enhance or accelerate natural processes to either boost carbon removal potential or improve storage durability. These methods can operate within either carbon cycle, depending on the approach. We'll look at enhanced weathering, ocean alkalinity enhancement, and biochar carbon removal. While these methods also benefit ecosystems, their primary goal is carbon removal.

The final group comprises engineered solutions that primarily operate in the slow carbon cycle. They are required because we only have a limited amount of resources available to us for the first two categories. Here, we'll delve into bioenergy with carbon capture and storage (beccs), direct air carbon capture and storage (DACCS), and two forms of CO_2 storage: underground and product-based, ideally in a durable way through mineralization.

This presentation of methods is by no means an exhaustive list of all possible forms of carbon removal. The field of Carbon Dioxide Removal is far too new and is developing at a rapid pace. In fact, it's quite possible that some of the most promising solutions for removing CO_2 are not even known yet. The methods we have selected are the most relevant today, and you'll likely encounter them as you explore CDR options for your company. At the end of the chapter, we'll also provide a classification of carbon removal and storage mechanisms, their respective benefits and challenges, as well as current and projected price points.

CHAPTER 4
LETTING NATURE DO THE HEAVY LIFTING

> "The carbon removal potential of nature is fantastic, but we will never achieve it if CO_2 is the only goal. If biodiversity and economic development are the goals, carbon removal will follow as a by-product."
>
> Tom Crowther, ecologist

Fancy a bet? We bet you've got one of the most effective carbon removal mechanisms around you right now. Don't believe it? Take a quick glance at your windowsill, out the window, or even at your plate. Chances are, you have spotted a plant in one – or all three – of those places. And in case you're currently sitting in a barren concrete jungle with no greenery in sight, don't worry. Even the paper this book is printed on has absorbed CO_2 at some point.

Photosynthesis is the magic word here – the almost miraculous process through which plants absorb and process CO_2, forming the basis of the fast carbon cycle. A significant portion of the CO_2 in our atmosphere gets absorbed by trees and crops. Crops typically have short lifespans, making their carbon removal effect temporary (think about that spinach your kids left on their plates, which will soon release most of its CO_2 back into the atmosphere as it decomposes). Trees, on the other hand, are different. They can live for decades, growing almost as large as a blue whale.

So, why not just plant trees everywhere? Goal achieved, net zero in sight – easy-peasy, right? Unfortunately, it's not quite that simple. On the following pages, we'll discuss why planting trees alone isn't enough, what other options exist to harness nature's photosynthesis power, and how your company should approach these methods.

> **In this chapter, we'll explore:**
>
> - how a range of carbon removal methods are based on photosynthesis and operate within the short carbon cycle,
> - why many seemingly simple solutions, like reforestation, hinge on specific, on-the-ground implementation,
> - what options your company has to engage in these methods, and why they should be viewed primarily as ecosystem restoration efforts rather than purely as carbon removal strategies.

Afforestation/Reforestation

The man who convinced none other than Donald Trump to plant a tree on the South Lawn of the White House is now sitting quietly in his Zurich office, letting out a sigh. Tom Crowther has had to recount this story more times than he can count, especially since the British *Guardian* published a major article about him in September 2021. The story says a lot about the current discourse on climate change solutions – and, unfortunately, not enough about the solutions themselves. "I would do things differently today," Crowther admits, explaining that his entire team will be undergoing media training immediately after our meeting to be better prepared for similar media storms in the future.

But let's rewind a bit. Crowther is a 37-year-old Welshman with a magnetic personality and boundless enthusiasm. After completing his PhD at Cardiff University, he embarked on an academic career

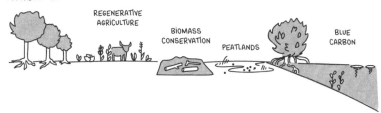

that took him to Yale. He first made headlines in 2015 – although primarily within the scientific community – when he published a study in the journal *Nature* that established the world's current tree population. According to the study, there are about 3 trillion trees on the planet – eight times more than previous estimates had suggested. This groundbreaking work quickly attracted the attention of some well-heeled Dutch patrons, who provided Crowther with up to 18.3 million USD in funding shortly after he joined Swiss university ETH Zurich as an assistant professor to establish a research group focused on studying the function and value of ecosystems.

The real splash, however, came in 2019. Together with his colleagues, Crowther published a study in the prestigious journal *Science* that estimated the Earth had enough space to plant an additional 1 trillion trees – an area roughly equivalent to the size of the United States. If these trees were planted and allowed to grow, the researchers calculated, they could absorb and store about 752 billion tons of CO_2 – around two-thirds of the 1,101 billion tons of CO_2 released into the atmosphere since the industrial revolution. The study led Crowther to declare in a press release: "Reforestation is the best solution we have today to combat climate change."

The study quickly garnered attention from both the scientific community and the media. According to *The Guardian*, it was the second most-cited climate change publication of 2019. Former U. S. Vice President Al Gore recommended it to Salesforce founder Marc Benioff, who helped launch the World Economic Forum's "1 Trillion

Tree Initiative," where companies and governments pledge to support the reforestation of a billion trees. Benioff reportedly described Crowther as the Steve Jobs of ecology [...] an ecopreneur."

A seemingly simple solution to such a complex problem as the climate crisis also found favor in the White House. At the 2020 World Economic Forum in Davos, then-President Donald Trump announced that the United States would participate in the initiative. A few months later, he and his wife Melania were photographed planting a tree to show their support.

However, the enthusiasm for the study was not universal. Criticism rained down from the scientific community. Crowther and his co-authors had used artificial intelligence to estimate the area available for planting, which included savannas and grasslands – ecosystems where significant tree growth is unlikely due to natural factors like fire and large grazing animals. The public communication of the study's results was also criticized. Several leading climate scientists labeled it "dangerously misleading," arguing that it suggested a single solution to climate change rather than a suite of essential actions, especially emission reductions.

"As an ecologist, when I talk about reforestation, I mean the holistic restoration of ecosystems. What journalists hear is: planting trees," Crowther reflects. "It took me a few months to understand this. It was clearly my mistake not to communicate more precisely. I should have made it clear that when we talk about nature's potential, we are definitely not talking about monocultures."

This episode highlights a broader issue in how we approach the climate crisis. Society and the media often latch onto a single solution and cling to it, like a mantra: "Just plant enough trees." But the reality is far more complex. From an ecological and carbon accounting perspective, the challenges are numerous.

What is clear, though, is that trees do absorb CO_2 from the atmosphere as they grow, storing it in their roots, trunks, and branches. There are three main ways to actively encourage this: afforestation (planting trees where none existed before), reforestation (planting trees in areas where forests were cut down), and natural regeneration (allowing ecosystems to recover with minimal human intervention).

The latter approach, while seemingly counterintuitive, is gaining traction. For example, the Bonn Challenge, launched in 2011, aims to restore 350 million hectares (865 million acres) of land by 2030. By 2024, nearly 60 nations had pledged a total of 210 million hectares (520 million acres). But it's not just about the quantity; the quality of restoration matters too.

In 2019, scientists estimated that 42 billion tons of carbon could be absorbed and stored if all 350 million hectares (865 million acres) were left to natural regeneration. However, if monocultures were planted instead, the potential drops to just 1 billion tons – a staggering 97 percent reduction.

When we think of forests, monocultures of oaks or pines are not what come to mind. Yet, they are surprisingly common, often because of their economic advantages. In 1974, Chile implemented a program that subsidized landowners to plant trees. But, as a study led by Robert Heilmayr of the University of California, Santa Barbara, shows, landowners often ended up cutting down existing forests to replace them with more profitable monocultures. The result was not only a failure to increase carbon removal but also a significant loss of biodiversity. This does not come as a surprise to Crowther: "The carbon removal potential of nature is fantastic, but we will never achieve it if CO_2 is the only goal. If biodiversity and economic development are the goals, carbon removal will follow as a by-product."

Other prominent examples illustrate why reforestation and afforestation are far from straightforward. In a large-scale reforestation project in China aimed at halting the spread of the Gobi Desert, up to 85 percent of the planted seedlings died because they were non-native species unsuited to the region. Similarly, in Turkey, the share of dead seedlings reached 90 percent, largely due to a lack of expertise – seedlings were planted at the wrong time of year and were not watered sufficiently. As *ScienceNews* journalist Carolyn Gramling points out, "There's too much focus on numbers of seedlings planted, and too little time spent on how to keep the trees alive in the long term, or in working with local communities."

Having learned from the 2019 study's shortcomings, Tom Crowther recently summoned a group of over 200 academics to provide an updated, ground-truthed assessment of the global carbon removal and storage potential of trees. Published in *Nature*, the study estimates that diverse, naturally recovering forests could capture around 829 gigatons of CO_2 in total, 61 percent of which comes from protecting existing forests and allowing them to mature, while the other 39 percent can be achieved by reconnecting fragmented landscapes through community-driven restoration.

In any case, carbon removal through forests comes with costs – whether for seedlings, planting, or forest management. Carbon credits are an established way to fund these projects, and an attractive one at that, with the price for 1 ton of CO_2 removed and stored ranging between 15 and 45 USD.

However, quality assurance can be challenging. For one, the additionality of these projects is not always clear, especially in the case of natural regeneration. How can a project prove what would have happened without the funding? This brings us back to the problem of the "counterfactual scenarios" that we discussed in Chapter 2 about the old carbon credit market.

Another clear issue is the risk of CO_2 re-emission. Carbon removal is only guaranteed for as long as the trees remain standing. However, the increasing frequency of forest fires, driven by the climate crisis, makes this less certain. In the summer of 2022, the U. S. nonprofit CarbonPlan published a study analyzing "California's Compliance Offset Program," which allows regulated firms to offset a certain percentage of their emissions by purchasing carbon credits instead of reducing their own emissions, typically with forestry credits. The carbon credits are backed by a "buffer pool" intended to insure against the risk of default and ensure CO_2 storage for 100 years – a concept we discussed in Chapter 2. The analysis showed that after just ten years, nearly 95 percent of the buffer pool put aside to protect against all fire risk for 100 years had already been used up due to devastating wildfires in the state. Even if these fires are still relatively rare in other regions, threats like bark beetles can also devastate forests.

Given these pitfalls and risks, should we just abandon reforestation and nature regeneration efforts? Absolutely not, says Tom Crowther, as long as we do it right: "Good restoration projects focus on economic empowerment and place the local community at the center as custodians of nature. After all, nobody greenwashes their own garden."

Crowther is now working on a software solution that is not too far removed from Steve Jobs' realm. The Restor platform uses Crowther's group's research, machine learning, and satellite imagery to transparently evaluate restoration projects worldwide – like a Google Maps for biodiversity. For example, Crowther can zoom in on his mother's garden in Cardiff, see which native species she could plant, and calculate the carbon removal potential. Whether Donald Trump's tree is still standing, however, is not documented. Nor is whether he was paid to plant it and ensure its survival.

As is often the case, the truth lies somewhere in the middle. Forestry carbon removal efforts are neither a panacea for the climate crisis nor a waste of money or mere greenwashing. When done correctly, they can significantly contribute to ecosystem restoration, economic development, and – albeit temporarily – remove a substantial amount of carbon dioxide from the atmosphere.

Regenerative Agriculture

Dressed in blue jeans, a black Patagonia jacket, and cowboy boots, Joko Winterscheidt rides a horse through a wild, hilly landscape bathed in that golden sunlight that can only be found on the American West Coast. In the background, the setting sun slowly sinks toward the horizon over the Pacific Ocean. Winterscheidt is one of Germany's most prominent TV personalities, having gained fame through a blend of celebrity interviews, absurd humor, and wild stunts – think of *Jackass meets The Tonight Show*. If you've followed his TV career, you might expect more of the absurd antics that made him famous – perhaps a beer marathon on horseback or mowing the lawn with children's scissors. But this time, you would be disappointed.

Instead, Winterscheidt is joined by a family of American farmers discussing how they manage their cattle in a sustainable and regenerative way. The farmers explain how they rotate the cattle frequently to prevent overgrazing, and Winterscheidt eagerly jumps in to help move the herd to the next field. This is all part of his project *The World's Most Dangerous Show*, a six-episode series that explores the consequences of and potential solutions to the climate crisis.

The camera pans to a row of happy cows basking in the sunlight and then to Winterscheidt riding his horse across the lush green hills. It is a picturesque scene of cowboy romance set against the backdrop of climate change, produced for none other than the online shopping giant Amazon – that's also part of the story. By the way, Winterscheidt cannot stop being silly after all: He gleefully pushes his cowboy boot into a horse's apple, grinning like a kid.

However, this romanticized image of agriculture is far from the reality for most farmers. Especially in the Global North, farming is a highly mechanized business with slim margins and immense financial pressure, dominated by large-scale monocultures and heavy use of artificial fertilizers. This hyper-intensive land use, aimed at maximizing short-term yields, has left soils around the world in a catastrophic state. Studies show that cultivated soils globally have lost 30 to 50 percent of the carbon stored in their upper layers compared to their natural state.

In the EU, as in the U. S., agricultural soils have actually become a net source of CO_2 rather than a sink. The disruption of natural cycles – where carbon and essential nutrients are taken up by plants, used, transformed, and eventually returned to the soil – has made agriculture, which accounts for around 12 percent of global greenhouse gas emissions, one of the biggest contributors to the climate crisis.

"Everyone agrees that agriculture could be regenerative," says Petrissa Eckle during our visit to Hoflabor, an innovative project at the pioneering SlowGrow farm near Zurich, Switzerland. "But we are just at the beginning of this innovation. We need machines, methods, and knowledge." Hoflabor – which translates to "Farm Laboratory" – is developing a particularly ambitious form of regenerative agriculture known as "mosaic farming." The goal is to create as much biodiversity as possible in and above the soil, enabling plants to grow productively without fertilizers and pesticides, while also sequestering carbon in the soil.

Petrissa Eckle is anything but your typical farmer. With a PhD in physics, she previously researched the effects of ultrashort laser pulses on atoms, worked for five years at management consultancy McKinsey & Company, and ran a sustainability think tank at ETH Zurich. Now, you can find her in rubber boots and a raincoat on an autumn day in the field. "Many of us are career changers, which sometimes helps us find fresh perspectives with a bit of naivety. Trained agronomists sometimes throw up their hands in disbelief, but it works," says Eckle.

The basic principles she and her team apply at Hoflabor are not new. The first researchers and practitioners began promoting the idea of regenerative agriculture in the 1980s, but its roots go much deeper, drawing on a range of indigenous practices designed to improve soil quality, biodiversity, and yields. These practices also enable the soil to absorb more CO_2.

The methods used include planting diverse crops throughout the year, integrating livestock into the fields, and rotating it frequently, as Winterscheidt discovered, or not plowing at all. Eckle explains further: "We try to disturb the soil as little as possible. The basic principle is that we only drive over the fields on fixed tracks, allowing loose, deep soil to develop between the tracks and an infrastructure of wormholes that remains intact for years. We also use minimal tillage, no plowing, and avoid weeding as much as possible, because all these activities disrupt the vibrant topsoil."

Instead, they rely heavily on mulch to cover the soil, especially when growing vegetables. "It helps control weeds, provides a buffer against heat, and feeds soil organisms – much like leaf fall in the forest. During Switzerland's last heatwave summer, while most potato growers suffered poor harvests, ours was well above average and of high quality – thanks largely to the mulch," says Eckle.

These practices not only ensure successful harvests but also enhance the soil's ability to sequester CO_2. Through photosynthesis, plants release CO_2 into the soil, where it is converted into organic compounds such as sugars. The exact mechanisms are still under debate, but it is thought that CO_2 is transported into the soil by plant roots or when plants die. Microorganisms also play a role, as does the conversion of organic compounds in the soil into a more stable form so-called "soil organic carbon," often referred to as "humus". If you are now thinking of chickpeas, olive oil, and flatbread, you might want to check the dictionary. What a difference an extra letter can make.

In addition to the additional absorption of atmospheric CO_2, regenerative agriculture has a number of other positive effects. For instance, these practices often require less heavy equipment, reducing reliance on fossil fuels. Natural soil improvement can also lower the need for energy-intensive artificial fertilizers. And, by not plowing, the carbon already stored in the soil remains there. This approach also helps reduce emissions of other potent greenhouse gases like methane and nitrous oxide.

While current research does not conclusively show that regenerative agriculture leads to higher yields, it does not indicate a reduction in yields either. Still, the number of farmers adopting these practices remains small, partly because the methods, while promising, are not fully mature. When asked by a *Science* journalist why he only selected his low-yielding fields to transition to regenerative practices, one Indiana farmer put it bluntly: "If it aligns with what I'm trying to already do and they want to pay me for it, more power to them," he says. "But I'm not going to risk my future and my kids' future."

Ivo Degn, the Austrian founder of Climate Farmers, a startup helping European farmers transition to regenerative agriculture, echoes this sentiment. Climate Farmers uses carbon credits to offset the financial risks for farmers, supporting them during the transition period. "Even though I don't think it is the ideal tool, it is the only one we have at the moment," says Degn. He believes that while farmers are interested in transitioning, they need financial support and better advice to reduce their risk.

Before a credit can be issued, it must be proven that carbon has actually been removed and stored. While regenerative management is known to increase soil organic carbon, accurately measuring this is time-consuming and costly. "The MRV process for high quality carbon credits can be almost prohibitively resource-intensive, so it only makes sense for a small group of farmers, which don't represent the majority of European farmers," says Degn. "Instead, I would love to simply pay farmers for their contributions to ecosystem services, but there is no mechanism for this."

The best method for assessing carbon removal involves taking soil samples and analyzing them in a lab. However, because agricultural soils are dynamic, open systems, even samples taken just a few meters apart can show vastly different carbon levels. "Soil carbon is intensely complicated," says Radhika Moolgavkar, former Vice President of Supply and Methodology at Nori, a carbon credit marketplace initially focused on regenerative agriculture projects. Citing a lack of demand for CDR credits, Nori, once considered one of the industry's early leaders, announced its closure in September 2024 (more on this in the Epilogue). To quantify carbon removal through regenerative practices accurately would require extensive sampling and analysis, Moolgavkar notes, "this is simply not economically feasible."

Today, it's common practice that computer models, combined with selective soil sampling, estimate the increase in a field's carbon content. One of the most established models is DayCent, originally developed at Colorado State University and used by major carbon crediting providers like Indigo and, in the past, Nori – despite a number of concerns around the uncertainty estimates of its carbon predictions and the lack of sufficient ground-truth verification data.

"We only employ the model on fields for which it has gone through a rigorous validation process, including independent, scientific review by an expert familiar with the model," says Max DuBuisson, Head of Impact and Integrity at Indigo, "this means we need to have enough data for the given combination of climate zone, soil type, crop and practice change to demonstrate model performance and quantify uncertainty." For instance, because they currently lack a sufficient amount of data related to changes in grazing practices, Indigo currently does not issue credits for this particular practice change. "It's a high, transparent bar," he adds.

Not everyone shares this optimistic view, though. Radhika Moolgavkar expresses a more cautious perspective: "I am not fully comfortable with the Measurement, Reporting, and Verification around soil carbon. It's incredibly nuanced and challenging to get right without significant resources – resources that, unfortunately, no one can afford." In her view, measuring and modeling carbon sequestration with sufficient certainty is a tough task. "Once we've determined how much carbon has been sequestered, monitoring it becomes easier."

While monitoring may be feasible, the risk of CO_2 escaping from the soil remains a significant challenge. The carbon is only stored as long as the practices are maintained. If the soil is disturbed, the stored CO_2 could be released back into the atmosphere. The easiest way to imagine this is through plowing: Much of the stored CO_2 is in the top 30 centimeters (1 foot) of the soil. If this is disturbed by a plow, these layers of soil are exposed to the atmosphere and the carbon can escape again. To mitigate this risk, contracts with project developers often require farmers to maintain these practices for a certain period. Europe-based Climate Farmers, for example, requires a commitment of ten years, while Indigo promises durability for 100 years.

In this context, Indigo's Max DuBuisson draws on a familiar analogy: "Think of an aggregated soil carbon project as a bank and the individual fields as bank accounts. Soil carbon in these fields is constantly in flux – there are deposits and withdrawals, and some fields might even be in the negative for a year. What is crucial is that at the project level, which in our case includes hundreds of farms and many thousands of fields, the deposits outweigh the withdrawals. Essentially, we are assessing: Is the bank healthy?" says DuBuisson. To ensure the promised 100-year durability, mechanisms such as vested payments for farmers, buffer pools, remote monitoring and insurances may be leveraged. Not everyone is on board with this promise, though. Soil scientist Jane Zelikova from Colorado State University shares her skepticism in an interview with *Science*: "The 100-year permanence isn't real."

Despite all these challenges, companies are still buying carbon credits from regenerative agriculture projects. One high-profile buyer is Microsoft, which in 2021 purchased 500,000 USD worth of carbon credits from projects including Australia's Wilmot Cattle Co. In the following years, regenerative agriculture projects continued to be part of its carbon removal portfolio, including CDR credits to be supplied by Indigo. One reason for this continued demand is cost: Credits are available for between 15 USD and 80 USD, significantly cheaper than those from more engineered solutions with longer storage periods.

As more farmers make the switch and regulatory pressure mounts, another aspect of carbon credits will come under closer scrutiny: additionality. If the U.S. and EU are serious about making regenerative agriculture central to their climate strategies, and subsidies or regulations follow, the transition to practices associated with CO_2 sequestration might occur without the need for financing through credits, making it difficult to issue them.

While there is still a long way to go, experts like Ivo Degn suggest that CDR credits may not be the perfect or permanent solution for driving the agricultural transition we so urgently need. However, they currently offer an opportunity to support pioneers in the agricultural system. This could be particularly interesting for companies in the food industry, whose business models depend on sustainably healthy soils. By integrating regenerative agriculture into their supply chains, companies can reduce their own emissions profiles – a practice known as insetting, as opposed to offsetting emissions with external carbon credits.

This approach appears to be gaining traction. As the *Financial Times* reported, 25 of the world's leading food and agribusiness companies, including household names such as Cargill, PepsiCo or Danone, strengthened their commitment to regenerative agriculture at COP28 in Dubai in December 2023. Together, they pledged to convert 65 million hectares (160 million acres) of land to regenerative practices and committed 2.2 billion USD in funding to support this transition in their supply chains. Nestlé has announced that half of its key ingredients will be sourced through regenerative agriculture by 2030. While these commitments are promising, when focused on carbon-related insetting outcomes, they face similar challenges as offsetting strategies.

Like reforestation, regenerative agriculture offers many benefits beyond carbon removal. However, the question remains: Is financing these activities through CDR credits the right path forward? Concerns around measurability and future additionality create uncertainty. At the same time, they might offer a mechanism to bridge the timespan until the agronomic benefits of practice changes materialize. From Petrissa Eckle's point of view, something else will be crucial for change: "As a farmer, I need methods and machines that work reliably and provide my crops with the best possible care. Biodiversity and humus formation are a means to this end for us, and this is a much greater motivation than credits, which have little financial weight compared to the harvest."

Peatlands

In the summer of 2018, the sleepy town of Meppen, Germany, became the unlikely epicenter of a major environmental disaster. What started as a routine missile test by the German army quickly spiraled out of control, resulting in a massive fire that ravaged the local peatlands. The blaze, which was initially sparked by military exercises, soon grew into a wildfire that consumed 8 square kilometers (3 square miles), releasing thick plumes of black smoke visible for miles. The district actually declared a state of emergency because the fire was so extremely difficult to control; it burned up to 1 meter (3 feet) into the ground in some places, and the carbon stored densely in the peatland kept feeding the fire.

Nearly 1,700 firefighters battled the inferno for weeks, but the real damage had already been done – both to the environment and the reputation of the German army. By the time the fire was extinguished, estimates suggested that between 800,000 and 1.4 million tons of CO_2 had been released into the atmosphere, equivalent to the annual emissions of two cement plants. The total cost of the operation and claims for damages amounted to 18.2 million USD.

The incident in Meppen briefly thrust peatlands into the spotlight, a rare occurrence for these often-overlooked ecosystems. Unlike the Amazon rainforests or the farmland around the corner, peatlands typically linger in the background, known more from literature and crime novels than from environmental discourse. As *The Washington Post* writer William Booth once quipped, "When bad things go down in Charles Dickens, the scene is set in a forbidding moor."

Yet, from a climate perspective, peatlands are anything but villains. In fact, their unique structure gives them an extraordinary ability to "pause" the short carbon cycle. When plant material such as leaves or roots fall into a peat bog, they decompose very slowly, if at all, thanks to the acidic, oxygen-free environment. This preserves the carbon they contain, locking it away in the form of peat. Over time, as new plants grow, die, and settle on top, a thick layer of carbon-rich material builds up – essentially forming a natural carbon sink. This process of biomass preservation has also inspired other methods of carbon removal, of which more later.

However, when these carbon-dense layers of peat catch fire, as they did in Meppen, they release massive amounts of CO_2 into the atmosphere. This is because peatlands store up to ten times more CO_2 than typical agricultural mineral soils. Globally, peatlands cover only about 10 percent of the Earth's surface but store twice as much CO_2 as all the world's forests combined. These vital ecosystems can be found in regions as diverse as Alaska, Europe, Russia, Canada, Congo, and the tropics.

Unfortunately, they are under threat: It is estimated that around 15 percent of the world's peatlands have already been lost, largely due to drainage for agricultural use and exploitation as soil substrate for private gardening. In the U.K., 87 percent of its peatland is now degraded or damaged; in Germany, the situation is even more dire, with 98 percent of the country's peatlands having been drained for development or farming.

When peatlands are drained, the preserved plant material is exposed to air, leading to decomposition and the release of stored CO_2. Scientists at the French Laboratory of Climate Sciences recently estimated that the conversion of peatlands to farmland could have released as much as 250 gigatons of CO_2 even before the industrial revolution – a staggering amount equivalent to five years of current global emissions. In the EU, drained peatlands are responsible for 220,000 tons of CO_2 emissions annually, accounting for 5 percent of the bloc's total emissions.

Given the massive amounts of carbon stored in peatlands and the potential for emissions if they dry out, researchers have rightfully dubbed these ecosystems a "carbon bomb"; a bomb that does not even need the German army's failed missile tests to cause immense CO_2 emissions – drying out is enough.

So, what can be done to defuse this carbon bomb? The most straightforward and effective method is rewetting, as without a natural inflow of water, peatlands would not have formed in the first place. Here, the main aim is to stop the water flowing out. "The first thing you have to do with a leaky spaceship is plug the hole," Richard Lindsay, a specialist in peatland ecosystems at the University of East London, explained to *The Washington Post*. By restoring the natural water levels in peatlands in this way, exposed layers of peat and dead biomass are submerged once again, halting further CO_2 emissions.

Crucially, this process highlights that rewetting is first and foremost about preventing emissions, not removing CO_2 from the atmosphere. Only when new plants grow, die, and are preserved in the peatland does active carbon removal occur. This distinction is critical when considering how to quantify the impact of peatland restoration. At present, accurately measuring carbon removal from peatlands is extremely challenging. The UK startup Sylvera recently received significant research funding to develop a solution to this very challenge. And the CDR market does not appear to be quite ready for carbon removal by peatlands either: While some initial methodologies exist for quantifying emission reductions through peatland rewetting, these only include the option for generating CDR credits as an afterthought.

There are also concerns about potential for methane emissions – a potent greenhouse gas – associated with the flooding of dried-up peatlands. Although the long-term climate benefits of CO_2 storage in peatlands are considered greater, these methane emissions have led some countries, like Denmark, to temporarily pause planned rewetting projects.

Overall, while peatlands offer immense potential as carbon sinks; they currently represent a massive source of emissions that need to be avoided rather than a rapidly scalable option for carbon removal. Their anaerobic environment does provide potential for long-term carbon storage, but the operationalization of this potential is still in its infancy. For the foreseeable future, peatlands are likely to remain more relevant to efforts in CO_2 avoidance and ecosystem restoration than in direct carbon removal.

Biomass Conservation

In the field of carbon removal, it has been said that the real challenge lies in capturing the CO_2, not storing it. And rightly so – imagine trying to pick out four red smarties from a bowl of 10,000 blue ones. But even when CO_2 is captured, the short lifespan of the fast carbon cycle means that the atmosphere quickly loses the fruits of its labor.

Peatlands have shown us a different way – a method to hit the pause button on this cycle. Taking inspiration from this, several new carbon removal techniques, collectively known as biomass conservation, are emerging with similar principles.

Picture the age of seafaring, long before the days of luxury cruise liners and their endless all-you-can-eat buffets. Sailors preparing for months-long ocean crossings faced the challenge of storing food without modern conveniences like refrigerators. They turned to a 4,000-year-old Indian tradition: preserving vegetables like cucumbers in brine, an oxygen-free environment that prevents spoilage by stopping the growth of harmful bacteria. Fast forward to today, and an Australian carbon removal startup is using a similar approach – but with a twist.

InterEarth is operating in parts of Australia where the soil has been heavily degraded by the clearing of native trees for agriculture. Without these large, water-absorbing trees, more rainwater evaporates under the harsh sun, leaving behind large quantities of salt – a process known as "secondary salinization." This salinized environment is ideal for InterEarth's method. They reforest the land with native species, then, once these trees reach a certain size, parts of each tree are harvested for conservation while the rest continues to grow. The woody biomass is then submerged in excavated pits filled with salty groundwater, sealed airtight, and covered with soil, effectively preserving the wood much like pickling vegetables.

"The key is creating an environment where the microorganisms that normally break down biomass do not thrive," explains Dr. Frauke Kracke, Science Lead at Frontier, a consortium of major companies including Stripe and Google's parent company Alphabet, which have collectively committed more than 1 billion USD to purchasing high-quality carbon removal credits.

A fortnight across the Pacific, another startup is working on a similar solution. In the western United States, where wildfires have ravaged landscapes, active forest management has become a critical part of climate strategies. Although it may sound counterintuitive, planned harvesting of selected sections of forest plays an important role in this process. Thinning removes the understory of the forest and cuts down trees to prevent fueling devastating fires. The problem is, this process generates a lot of wood, which is often left to rot or burned – releasing and thereby "wasting" the CO_2 it had absorbed back into the atmosphere. Enter Kodama Systems, a startup with a simple yet innovative solution called the "wood vault."

Kodama's approach involves digging a hole, lining it with a special Geotex liner (a type of plastic film), and filling it with the biomass. Once sealed, the hole is filled with soil and planted to prevent re-wetting as, unlike for InterEarth, non-saline water would accelerate decomposition in the vault. What both approaches have in common is that the oxygen-free environment prevents decomposition.

Kodama's first facility is currently under permitting and development in Nevada. "Additionally, two- and five-year, small scale burial experiments have been installed by the Carbon Containment Lab [a nonprofit research group spun out of Yale University] in Colorado," explains Jimmy Voorhis, Head of Biomass Utilization and Policy at Kodama. One of the aims of these trials is to prove that the carbon remains firmly stored in the biomass – for how long and how safely.

Indeed, it is one of the key challenges for both InterEarth and Kodama, as well as other CDR companies pursuing biomass conservation, to prove the long-term durability of this CDR method. "Theoretical storage times are promising, but there always is the risk that extreme weather or human activity could disturb these sites, releasing the stored carbon back into the atmosphere," explains Kracke. For example, a flood could disrupt the saline environment in InterEarth's pits, or future land use changes could lead to the excavation of Kodama's biomass storage sites.

Despite these uncertainties, companies are already investing in these methods. InterEarth's first major customer is Klarna, the Swedish financial services company, which has committed to supporting the removal of up to 13,686 tons of CO_2 with a guaranteed durability of 100 years, certified by the CDR standard puro.earth. This procurement is one of the larger ones in the nascent carbon removal market, accounting for more than half of Klarna's carbon credit portfolio.

Overall, the feasibility of these methods is still being debated. Some experts suggest alternative approaches, such as lining the wood vaults with clay instead of plastic or preserving biomass using cold rather than salt or dehumidification. Kracke does not think this is too far-fetched: "Anything that makes our food last longer could theoretically be used for this approach." Sinking biomass in oxygen-free water is another idea, inspired by the perfectly preserved wooden ships found in certain parts of the ocean. "We know it works," says Kracke, "but these approaches are still in their infancy."

As with all biomass carbon removal methods, the success of these initiatives depends on the availability of sustainable biomass sources and the involvement of local communities. Forest thinning, for example, is sometimes met with resistance from environmental groups. In California local NGOs managed to halt one such project by the State Forestry Department, highlighting the importance of involving communities to address concerns around the sustainability of the biomass used.

There also is the issue of nutrient removal, which, while not an immediate concern, could become significant as these methods scale up. Biomass not only sequesters atmospheric CO_2 but also contains essential nutrients like nitrate and phosphorus, which are removed from the ecosystem when the biomass is stored. "Ultimately, it is about finding the best use for the biomass from a holistic perspective," Kracke concludes. "In some cases, conservation might be the best option; in others, it might make more sense to use the biomass for biochar or bioenergy with carbon capture and storage. This also depends on future costs."

If the assumptions about the longevity of carbon storage prove correct, biomass conservation could become a highly sought-after CDR method. Although prices are currently high – U.S. buyer initiative Frontier, for instance, agreed on a purchase option with Kodama Systems at 610 USD per ton – there is potential for these approaches to become more cost-effective as the technology scales and the premium paid to measure, report and verify the carbon removal reliably is decreased. The signing of a three-year offtake deal by Frontier with U.S. biomass conservation startup Vaulted Deep in April 2024, priced at 380 USD per ton of CO_2 removed, already indicated the cost reduction potential of the CDR method.

Cost points below 100 USD per ton are certainly within reach, especially if the uncertainties can be further reduced and the technology scaled up. It will be interesting to see how high the costs of sourcing, transporting, and actually storing biomass on a large scale will ultimately be. Of course, any emissions generated here must be subtracted from the removal performance in a comprehensive Life Cycle Assessment (LCA) (more on this method in the next chapter).

Unlike many of the carbon removal methods in the short carbon cycle discussed in this chapter, biomass conservation holds significant potential as a pure carbon removal strategy. While it may not offer additional environmental benefits, it promises to sequester CO_2 effectively and affordably for long periods of time. The key to its success will be securing sustainable biomass sources and answering important questions about the durability of carbon storage before it can be implemented on a large scale.

Blue Carbon

Every October, the United Nations Office in Kenya presents the Person of the Year Award to recognize outstanding contributions to society and the environment. In 2021, the honor went to the founder of a nutrition program for schoolchildren, and in 2022, an agronomist was celebrated for his work in regenerative agriculture. Photographs show both laureates proudly holding a framed certificate emblazoned with the blue UN logo.

But in 2023, the award required a wider lens – literally. That year, the Person of the Year was not an individual but an entire project: Mikoko Pomaja, which means "mangroves together" in Swahili. And it was this idea of community that the UN emphasized in its citation as a "beacon of hope" and a shining example of the power of community engagement and innovation.

Mikoko Pomaja is no stranger to accolades. It was the world's first blue carbon project financed by the sale of carbon credits and has often been highlighted by the United Nations Development Programme as a model for successful community-based environmental efforts. It even was one of the 15 winners of the 2017 Equator Prize.

So, what exactly is blue carbon? In simple terms, it refers to carbon stored in marine and coastal ecosystems – hence the "blue" in the name. These ecosystems include mangrove forests, seagrass beds, and tidal marshes near the coast – areas that are irrigated and drained by the ebb and flow of the tide, also known as coastal wetlands. In the open sea, there are seaweed and algae projects.

Blue carbon approaches are among the most efficient CO_2 absorption and storage systems on the planet, capable of removing CO_2 from the atmosphere up to three times faster and storing three to five times more CO_2 than tropical rainforests. Despite covering only 0.5 percent of the seafloor, blue carbon ecosystems are responsible for up to 50 percent of the organic carbon stored in the seabed.

The secret to their efficiency lies in their rapid growth and the oxygen-poor, anaerobic conditions they thrive in – conditions that slow down carbon decomposition and extend storage times, much like peatlands. These ecosystems are also remarkably resilient, able to withstand significant temperature fluctuations and changes in water salinity.

But the benefits of blue carbon ecosystems go far beyond just carbon storage. Dr. James Kairo, a senior scientist at the Kenya Marine and Fisheries Research Institute and one of the initiators of the Mikoko Pomaja project, considers them central: "The other benefits of mangroves are far greater than the value of the carbon credits," he said in a webinar hosted by the World Resource Institute (WRI).

A study by Stanford University researchers, published in the prestigious journal *Nature*, backs this up. The study estimated the value of protecting 64,000 hectares (158,000 acres) of mangrove forest in Belize, Africa, at more than 3.5 million USD per year in tourism revenue and lobster stocks for local fisheries. Planting an additional 13,000 hectares (32,000 acres) could add another 5 million USD to the economy.

Equally important is the role these ecosystems play in protecting coastal communities from the immediate impacts of the climate crisis. The same study found that protecting and expanding mangrove forests could halve the number of people exposed to flash floods and other coastal hazards. Mangroves, with their complex root systems, act as natural buffers, absorbing the energy of storms and reducing the hazard risk. They also prevent seawater from contaminating vital drinking water resources during storms and floods. The main protective function of seagrass is to reduce erosion in coastal areas by compacting and stabilizing the soil through its deep roots.

Despite their immense value, the current state of blue carbon ecosystems is alarming. In the WRI webinar, Lisa Schindler Murray, Director of Natural Climate Solutions at the U. S. conservation organization Rare, highlights that "about 50 percent of tidal marshes, 35 percent of mangrove forests, and 29 percent of seagrass beds have been lost since the mid-20th century." In some cases, these ecosystems are disappearing at rates four times faster than tropical rainforests.

To secure these critical carbon reservoirs and restore those that have been lost, conservation and restoration are essential. From a carbon perspective, these activities, as well as other short carbon cycle projects, serve two distinct functions: Conserving existing blue carbon helps avoid the release of CO_2 already stored, while restoration – such as planting new mangroves or seagrass – leads to additional CO_2 absorption and storage. Both are vital, but only restoration actively removes CO_2 from the atmosphere.

Similar to other approaches to carbon removal based on photosynthesis in ecosystems, demonstrating and quantifying the benefits of blue carbon projects poses a number of challenges. Research shows that CO_2 storage in these ecosystems can vary dramatically. For example, CO_2 storage in sediment – an important indicator of carbon removal – can vary by a factor of 600 in tidal marshes, 76 in seagrass beds, and 19 in mangroves. This is a problem because it is not economically or practically feasible to quantify CO_2 sequestration using actual soil samples. Instead, models are used which do not yet appear to be sufficiently backed up by well-founded assumptions – with the result that in some cases, the results still vary widely.

The more impractical it is to actually measure plant growth or CO_2 uptake, the greater the challenge. While project staff at Mikoko Pomaja can track newly planted mangroves, it is much harder to do so in the open ocean. Still, there is potential for blue carbon projects offshore.

However, unlike coastal approaches, the plants here do not grow rooted in the seabed – at depths of over 200 meters (650 feet) there is hardly enough light for photosynthesis – but float on the surface. We are talking about algae and seaweed. As they grow, they absorb CO_2 stored in the ocean; the ocean then comes into equilibrium with the atmosphere, taking CO_2 out of the atmosphere to restore the balance (more on this in Chapter 5). When wind, weather, waves or human intervention cause parts of the algae to break off, they sink to the seabed, where they are stored for the long term as part of the sediment.

This approach was once seen as highly promising because seaweed and algae grow rapidly – some up to 60 centimeters (2 feet) per day! – and their cultivation does not compete for land used for food production. However, recent concerns have tempered this enthusiasm. Experts worry that large-scale cultivation could disrupt existing marine ecosystems. Algae, for example, could compete with phytoplankton, which forms the basis of marine food chains and is already a crucial part of the carbon cycle. "This is a major threat to the biosecurity of the ocean," warns Philip Boyd, a professor of marine biogeochemistry at the University of Tasmania, in an interview with *MIT Technology Review*.

The journey of seaweed cultivation and sinking as a carbon removal strategy can be illustrated by the story of Running Tide, a startup originated in Maine on the U.S. East Coast. Once hailed as a shining example of the budding CDR industry, the company launched with a straightforward yet ambitious plan: to deploy floating buoys to the open ocean, each equipped with long strands teeming with seaweed and kelp seedlings, nourished by a nutrient mix designed to fuel their growth. As the seaweed grew, it would absorb CO_2, and once it reached a certain size, the strands would be cut, allowing the kelp to sink to the ocean floor where it would be sequestered for the long term.

It was this very operation, planned off the coast of Maine, that caught the attention of researcher Boyd. In a 2022 paper, he highlighted a range of potential ecological risks, including changes to water chemistry and the microbial balance. In part as a response to the challenges they encountered, Running Tide pivoted its approach, relocating much of its operations to Iceland. There, they began sinking bundles of wood chips coated with alkaline material into the coastal waters. Coating the biomass with alkaline lime kiln dust was intended to prevent acid leaching into the water; Running Tide later said it was also done for another carbon removal purpose: increasing ocean alkalinity (more on this in Chapter 5). Since 2022, they have reportedly sunk 19,000 tons of wood chips off the Iceland coast.

The company's initial track record seemed promising: 25,000 tons of CO_2 removed, 21,000 CDR credits delivered to high-profile buyers like Microsoft and Shopify, and significant venture capital funding secured, including 54 million USD fresh capital in 2022. However, despite these early successes, CEO Martin Odlin announced in June 2024 that Running Tide would be shutting down its operations and laying off all employees, citing a lack of demand for their credits in the voluntary market. His statement did not delve into the other challenges faced by blue carbon projects – be it the uncertainties around ecological effects of large scale deployments, the unresolved questions around MRV or long and complicated permitting processes – but it is likely they played a significant role in the company's downfall.

Given these risks, it is crucial that blue carbon projects are rigorously verified against established standards, and that carbon credits are only issued when there is a demonstrable CO_2 benefit. Because proving this benefit is more difficult in blue ecosystems, the price of blue carbon credits is generally higher than for traditional land-based forestry projects, ranging from 20 USD to 60 USD per ton.

As with many other carbon removal methods in the short carbon cycle, at least part of the value of blue carbon projects lies in their positive effects on ecosystems. This is particularly true for blue carbon, as mangroves, seagrass beds, and tidal marshes form a literal first line of defense against the immediate impacts of the climate crisis. They protect coastlines and local communities. From a carbon removal perspective, however, challenges remain. Although the durability of CO_2 storage in these ecosystems is generally greater than in afforestation projects, it is still limited and vulnerable to temperature fluctuations and extreme weather events.

For Those in a Hurry

	Afforestation	Regenerative Agriculture	Peatlands	Biomass Conservation	Blue Carbon
Carbon removal and storage mechanism	Capture by photosynthesis, storage in roots, trunk, and branches	Capture by photosynthesis, storage as organic carbon in the soil	Capture by photosynthesis, storage through dead biomass in anoxic environments	Capture by photosynthesis, storage in an artificially created environment that prevents decomposition	Capture by photosynthesis, storage in plant biomass in anoxic environments
Price per ton of CO_2 removed	15–45 USD	15–80 USD	no data	today: 380–650 USD prospectively: <100 USD	20–60 USD
Advantages	Positive co-benefits for ecosystems, biodiversity, and local communities	Significant positive impacts on yields, soil health & ecosystems; emission reductions	Significant source of emissions that can be avoided by known means	High durability, MRV solvable	Solid to high durability, depending on approach; protection of ecosystems against effects of climate crisis
Challenges	Limited durability threatened by extreme weather; incentives for monoculture plantations	Limited durability, economic measurability of CO_2 storage; decreasing additionality with an increase in practices	Currently hardly to operationalize as carbon removal project	No co-benefits; risk of nutrient removal; unresolved scientific questions	Durability threatened by extreme weather; ecosystem impacts unclear in some approaches

CHAPTER 5
LENDING NATURE A HELPING HAND

> "Nature doesn't need people –
> people need nature."
>
> Harrison Ford, actor and environmental activist

A late summer morning in County Wicklow, Ireland. Wicklow is just a 30-minute drive from the hustle and bustle of Dublin's city center, but it feels like a world apart. The gray concrete jungle of the Irish capital gives way to the lush greenery of Wicklow Mountain National Park, a place so vital to the city's air quality that it is often called "the lungs of Dublin."

As you would expect on a September day in Ireland, a light mist blankets the ground, accompanied by a gentle but persistent rain. The horizon is dotted with fields of barley – golden, swaying, and destined to become one of Ireland's most iconic exports: Guinness beer. Flanking the barley fields are verdant meadows where cows graze contentedly, their image ready to grace any ad for Irish dairy products.

It's a quintessential Irish scene, and even 33-year-old Maurice Bryson and his colleague Leo Hickey seem reluctant to disturb the peace. Clad in rubber boots, the pair moves through the countryside, using an oversized corkscrew to extract soil samples. Hickey, equipped with a rain jacket and trousers, seems ready for the weather. Bryson, on the other hand, is in shorts, a polo shirt, and a waistcoat. When asked if he's cold, he simply shrugs, "You get used to it." Later tonight, he will swim a few kilometers in the sea – sans wetsuit, naturally.

A few weeks earlier, two hours south in County Wexford, you might have spotted the duo aboard a tractor, methodically crisscrossing the fields. The ground there looked parched, with photos capturing clouds of gray-brown dust trailing behind the tractor. But Bryson quickly corrects any assumptions. "That is concrete powder, not dust," he explains. "We spread leftover concrete from construction sites across the fields. It is standard in the industry to order more concrete than you need – we just put that excess to good use." And one of the only other sensible uses – recycling concrete – is often economically challenging.

Concrete? The very same building material responsible for 8 percent of global CO_2 emissions? In a field? Should you still feel good about that sandwich with Irish butter and a pint of Guinness? Bryson nods confidently, "Concrete has some surprising benefits for the soil. It can optimize pH levels, release valuable nutrients, make plants more resilient, and boost productivity. And most importantly for our discussion, it can absorb CO_2 from the atmosphere and lock it away safely for the long term."

What Bryson is describing is one example from a toolkit of carbon removal methods where humans are lending a hand to nature's own processes, speeding up the rate at which carbon dioxide is safely removed from the atmosphere. On the following pages, we'll delve into three of the most important techniques: enhanced weathering, ocean alkalinity enhancement, and biochar carbon removal.

In this chapter, we'll explore:

- how these carbon removal methods work in detail,
- the pros and cons of each method, and when they might start making a significant contribution to carbon removal,
- how you, as a business leader, can incorporate these methods into your climate strategies, both now and in the future.

Enhanced Weathering

Like Petrissa Eckle, Maurice Bryson does not exactly fit the classic image of a farmer. With his long, slicked-back hair, you might expect the 33-year-old to be more at home on the trading floor in a sharp suit rather than in rubber boots on a tractor. And for a long time, you would have been right. Bryson's journey took him through universities in St Andrews and Edinburgh, followed by a stint at a major financial services company in London's notorious City.

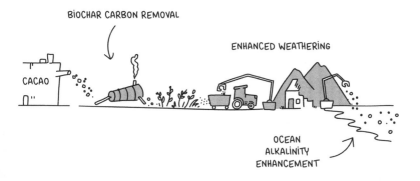

But the pull of the land never quite let him go. Even while studying, he kept one foot in agriculture, working part-time in the field. This connection eventually led him to trade the concrete jungle for actual fields. In 2022, together with Frank McDermott, a geochemist from University College Dublin, Bryson founded Silicate – a startup that is part of a growing movement using nature's own mechanisms to tackle the excess of carbon dioxide in our atmosphere.

Silicate's approach taps into a natural process that, along with photosynthesis (which we covered in the previous chapter), helps regulate Earth's CO_2 levels: the weathering of rocks. This natural process plays a key role in maintaining our planet's delicate balance – keeping our atmosphere at a livable 0.04 percent CO_2, rather than spiraling into a Venus-like 96 percent CO_2 hellscape, where temperatures hover around a toasty 400 degrees Celsius (750 degrees Fahrenheit).

Let's bring it back to Earth. When rain falls, it picks up CO_2 from the atmosphere, becoming slightly acidic as it makes its way to the ground. But before you start worrying about acid rain from the 70s and 80s, relax – thanks to advances in pollution control, today's rainwater is more akin to fizzy water. And what gives it that fizz? It is the CO_2, reacting with water to form carbonic acid.

Now, when this slightly acidic rain meets alkaline rocks – whether they are part of a mountain, a stone, or even concrete – a slow chemical reaction begins. The CO_2 in the rainwater reacts with the minerals in these alkaline materials, breaking them down and transforming the CO_2 into bicarbonates. These bicarbonates stay in the water for hundreds of thousands of years.

"You can think of the process as a game of Pac-Man: The acidity of the CO_2 eats away at the alkaline material. What comes out at the end of Pac-Man is bicarbonate," says Bryson, "that's how I explain it to my parents." The water, enriched with CO_2 and minerals, then flows through groundwater into rivers and eventually the ocean, where the CO_2 is stored safely for the long term as bicarbonate and later as limestone on the ocean floor.* "The Alps, for example, consist entirely of limestone, which means that an incredible amount of CO_2 is stored there," says Dr. Maria-Elena Vorrath, who researches enhanced weathering at the University of Hamburg.

From nature's perspective, this weathering process is a bit like a thermostat, keeping the Earth's CO_2 levels and temperature in check. The catch? It is a slow process – painfully slow. Each year, natural weathering removes about 1 gigaton of CO_2 from the atmosphere. To put that in perspective, that is about the same amount of CO_2 we currently emit in just nine days. If we were to stop all emissions today, it would take roughly 1,500 years to pull all the CO_2 we've emitted since the industrial age out of the atmosphere. And time is something we don't have in the fight against the climate crisis.

The natural process is limited by surface area – only the outer layer of rock or material can react with rainwater, much like how Pac-Man can only munch on the dots directly in front of him. But break the rock into smaller pieces, and you dramatically increase the surface area, speeding up the weathering process. Just like crushed ice melts faster than a solid cube, pulverized rock weathers much quicker than a whole mountain. In this way, a process that would normally take thousands of years can be reduced to a few months or years.

This is where Silicate comes in. Rather than dumping tons of concrete blocks onto fields, they use finely ground concrete powder, with particles small enough to give every bit of material a chance to react with carbonated rainwater. That is one part of the acceleration.

The second is that the rain does not stop absorbing CO_2 just because it has reached the ground. As described in Chapter 4, agricul-

---

* In addition to storing CO_2 as bicarbonate, depending on the material and environment, the CO_2 also reacts to form calcium carbonate, which remains in the soil in the long term. However, this form of CO_2 sequestration is less effective and therefore negligible.

tural soils are enriched with carbon dioxide, at peak levels up to 60 times more concentrated than in the atmosphere. The water thus has the opportunity to absorb even more CO_2, which can then react with the alkaline powder in the upper layers of the soil.

On a good day, Silicate spreads around 200 tons of this powder across the fields. "That lets us remove a conservative estimate of 20 tons of CO_2," says Bryson. 20 tons – that is a drop of acidic rain in the ocean, compared to the multiple gigatons of carbon removal that the IPCC estimates we'll need mid-century. For context, to remove just 1 gigaton of CO_2 annually, we'd need to spread 1 to 5 gigatons of weatherable materials like basalt or concrete each year. The construction industry, by comparison, produces 30 gigatons of concrete yearly – though only a small fraction of that ever gets returned for reuse.

Clearly, scaling up will require a lot of material. "It won't fail due to a lack of raw materials," says Dr. Cara Maesano. The physicist heads the geochemical carbon removal unit at the U.S. think tank RMI and recently published a review of the potential of accelerated weathering and mineralization. In her mind, surface and underground deposits are sufficient for much larger quantities of carbon removal. In particular because apart from concrete, basic rocks such as basalt or olivine-bearing dunite could also be used. However, she cautions that transporting and grinding these materials to micrometer size requires energy, which generates emissions that must be factored into the overall net carbon removal.

This is where Life Cycle Assessment (LCA) comes in – a critical tool in the carbon removal space. LCA looks at the environmental impacts, such as emissions and water use, of a product or service from the beginning to the end of its life, including sourcing, production, use, and disposal or recycling. When it comes to carbon removal, all the emissions generated in the process must be subtracted from the CO_2 removed to get the net removal value.

This need for precise calculations and reliable proof of carbon removal explains why companies like Silicate are still working on a relatively small scale. "Because we are putting our material into a very open system like agricultural soils, it is challenging to measure and prove CO_2 uptake reliably and accurately," explains Silicate founder Bryson. But this proof is essential for issuing credits that companies can buy to offset their emissions. As a result, many startups in this field are heavily investing in scientific research and field trials to reduce uncertainties.

Silicate, for example, recently moved into a new office near University College Dublin, complete with scientific equipment worth hundreds of thousands of dollars. Pointing to an oversized suction cup, Bryson explains, "We can use this to measure the CO_2 and other greenhouse gases flowing in and out of the soil." This is particularly important for their work with concrete, as its high reactivity is both a blessing and a curse. "In the right soil, concrete can bind CO_2 quickly and effectively. But if the soil is over-fertilized, it might release more CO_2 than it captures," Bryson notes. Dr. Maria-Elena Vorrath from the University of Hamburg confirms this: "Every soil is different. We sometimes have soil samples 20 meters (65 feet) apart that show completely different potential for CO_2 storage." That's why, Bryson says, Silicate is still very much focused on research and is also using other materials such as limestone.

Shantanu Agarwal knows a thing or two about the diversity in soils. As the founder of Mati Carbon, an enhanced weathering company active in India and Africa, Agarwal's agricultural partners are not operating on vast, 100-hectare farms like their counterparts in Europe or North America. Instead, he collaborates with a massive number of subsistence farmers in the Global South, where typical landholdings are about 1 hectare (2.5 acres) per farmer. "There are 200 million of these farmers in the Global South who could benefit from the positive effects of weathering on their soils, along with the increased income from improved crop productivity and carbon removal credits," he explains. Because of the small plot sizes and varied farming practices, Agarwal has to put extra effort into measuring the effects on these soils. "Our extensive high-density sampling has given us a better understanding of the heterogeneity of our soils than the typical weathering companies in the Global North."

Born in India and educated in the U.S., Agarwal is one of a few people with some mileage in the young CDR industry. A former oil and gas engineer turned venture capital investor, he first founded Sustaera, a direct air capture company, in 2019. However, a trip to India opened his eyes to the realities of subsistence farming and the immediate impacts of the climate crisis on farmers' livelihoods. "I knew about weathering, did more research, tested soil and rock samples – and it checked out: India is warm, with plentiful alkaline rock supply, and the soils are a perfect fit."

Two years later, his company Mati Carbon – a rare, nonprofit controlled startup – has grown to 60 employees and works with more than 10,000 partner farmers. By the end of 2024, they will have spread 100,000 tons of basalt in India. "That will lead to 20,000 to 30,000 tons of carbon removal," Agarwal explains, "but more importantly, it will significantly improve crop yields and soil health for thousands of farmers. This is how we get farmers on board." For Agarwal, putting farmers first is also key to ensuring that carbon removal in the Global South does not become yet another case of the Global North exploiting resources. "We cannot eliminate that risk entirely, but we need to show we have learned from the mistakes of the past."

At the far end of Silicate's lab in Dublin, a large workbench is cleared for a robot that will soon be analyzing hundreds of water samples each week for bicarbonate content – a task that would otherwise require a full-time employee. For Bryson, this capability is crucial because direct measurement of bicarbonate is the preferred method to confirm carbon removal. Dr. Vorrath agrees: "Measuring bicarbonate directly is the best and most reliable solution. However, it turns out that this is much more difficult in the field than in the laboratory, because there are simply too many influencing factors. It is currently unclear whether we will be able to solve this issue completely." A range of entrepreneurs have realized this bottleneck for the success of enhanced rock weathering and have started to develop and commercialize devices for efficient in-field measurement.

Silicate's field tests and analyses also aim to assess the environmental impact of their materials. When concrete or other alkaline materials come into contact with rainwater, all components, including potentially harmful ones that farmers do not want on their fields, break down. For instance, some olivine-rich rocks contain heavy metals like nickel, which could be released more quickly due to accelerated weathering. "We need more data to make a final assessment of the potential risks," says Vorrath. Concrete, of course, could also be mixed with other materials that do not necessarily belong on agricultural soils. However, Bryson reassures that Silicate checks for a range of metals and other undesirable materials before spreading them.

Despite the uncertainties, Silicate has already attracted customers, including the Swedish financial services company Klarna. Similarly, InPlanet, a German-Brazilian startup spreading basalt rock on Brazilian fields, has secured backing from Frontier, a consortium led by tech giants like Stripe and Alphabet. In late 2023, Frontier also inked its first long-term offtake deal in enhanced weathering with U. S. West Coast-based Lithos Carbon, procuring 154,240 tons of carbon removal for about 57 million USD.

One reason for this interest is the long-term potential of accelerated weathering to remove large amounts of CO_2 at a competitive price. Today, Silicate's cost of removing and storing 1 ton of CO_2 is around 440 USD. But Bryson believes this could drop to 165 to 220 USD in the future, potentially even below 110 USD if farmers contribute to the cost of the material.

That said, these price predictions come with caveats. There are still many unknowns, particularly regarding the cost of verification and scaling material sourcing. This uncertainty is reflected in the wide range of price estimates: Some studies suggest prices between 80 and 275 USD per ton by 2050, while current prices vary from 270 USD to 800 USD, depending on factors like project location, material type, and proof of removal accuracy. The average price hovers around 370 USD which is also the price tag of Frontier's offtake deal with Lithos.

Despite these challenges, experts agree that accelerated weathering is one of the most promising carbon removal methods. It is scalable and offers long-term CO_2 storage on a geological timescale. Plus, its benefits for farmland make it particularly appealing to buyers in the food industry as well as geographies in the Global South with high densities of subsistence agriculture. However, before scaling up, it is crucial to answer the remaining questions and establish reliable methods for Measuring, Reporting, and Verifying carbon removal.

Dr. Vorrath sums it up: "I think there are enough reasons to take action now, as long as we quantify the uncertainties. Then, only the part where we can prove carbon removal with certainty will be sold. And as we reduce those uncertainties, the amount we can sell will increase. So, you could tell buyers, 'You can now get X amount for Y price' – and if our research shows we have been too cautious, you will end up getting even more."

Ocean Alkalinity Enhancement

The next carbon removal method whisks us away from the serene Irish autumn to a classic summer holiday picture of sunbathers basking on hot sands, kids splashing in the waves, and the air filled with the familiar mix of sunscreen and crisps. It is a time of carefree relaxation, where worries about the climate or the future security of your employer feel as distant as the horizon, let alone the connection between the two. But in the future, one of the solutions to our CO_2 woes might be lying right beneath your beach towel on the shores of the North Sea or the Gulf of Mexico.

Enter Project Vesta, a startup from the U.S. with a big vision: turning many of the world's coastlines into carbon removal zones. Their method is called "Ocean Alkalinity Enhancement," (OAE) and it works on the same principle as accelerated weathering – just without the detour through farmlands. The idea is simple: Take a suitable material, like the mineral olivine, grind it down to the size of sand grains, and spread it along the coast.

The inspiration for this method comes from a place high on any geochemist's bucket list: Papakolea Beach in Hawaii. If you google pictures of this beach, you might do a double-take. The deep green color of the sand looks like a lush Irish meadow melting into the sea. But look closer, and you will see it is not grass, it is green sand. This unique color comes from olivine-rich lava that flowed into the bay during a 19th-century eruption of the Papakolea volcano. Now, before you start worrying about the iconic white beaches on your next holiday postcards, rest assured – when olivine is spread for carbon removal, it blends with the existing white sand, so no one is the wiser about the green stuff.

Once on the beach, the mineral is washed out to sea by the tide and surf, saving the cost and effort of distributing it directly in the open ocean. The tides also naturally grind the mineral down further, speeding up its reaction with the CO_2 dissolved in the ocean. The ocean, after all, is one of the world's largest CO_2 reservoirs, already absorbing nearly a third of the world's CO_2 without any help from us. The same weathering process we discussed on land happens here, too, turning CO_2 into bicarbonates that safely lock it away for the long term.

"It's actually pretty straightforward," says Dr. Antonius Gagern. "When atmospheric carbon is absorbed by the ocean, it gradually transforms into carbonate and bicarbonate. How much of each depends largely on the pH of the water. The more alkaline the water, the more bicarbonate; the more acidic, the more CO_2. It's a bit like air: When it's warm, it can hold more moisture, but cool it down, and that moisture falls as rain." Gagern, who leads the Carbon to Sea Initiative, a nonprofit organization focused on researching marine carbon removal, has always had a deep connection to the ocean – whether studying marine biology, earning a PhD in fisheries economics, or catching waves in his spare time. We caught up with him in Berlin after a business trip to the U.S. West Coast, where he naturally squeezed in a few hours of surfing in the Pacific.

Back to the method of increasing ocean alkalinity: The actual removal of CO_2 from the atmosphere happens after the material reacts in the ocean, because the initial reaction only affects CO_2 already dissolved in the water. The crucial step is what comes next: The ocean and atmosphere are constantly exchanging CO_2, striving to maintain equilibrium. When rock particles near the coast react with CO_2 in the water to form bicarbonate, they create capacity for the ocean to absorb more atmospheric CO_2 to restore balance.

To picture this, imagine a sunny day on Lake Tahoe. When the sun finally makes an appearance, locals and tourists flock to the water – prime time for renting a canoe. And what is a canoe without the oversized sponge, reminiscent of school days spent avoiding to present your math homework by wiping the blackboard?

Now, let's say the weather turns, and rain starts to fill your canoe. Time to put that sponge to use! But if it is already soaked, dipping it into the growing puddle in the boat will not help. You need to wring it out first. Once it is dry again, you can finally soak up the water and keep the canoe afloat.

In simple terms, this is what happens with ocean alkalization. The ocean acts like a sponge for atmospheric CO_2, but once it is

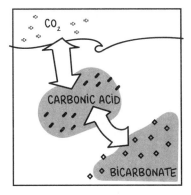 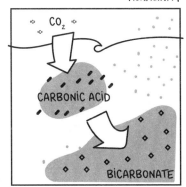

Illustration based on original by Ocean Visions

saturated, it cannot absorb any more.* This is where our carbon removal method comes in: By reacting rock particles with CO_2 in the water to form bicarbonate, we are essentially wringing out the sponge, making room for more CO_2 from the atmosphere until balance is restored. Gagern has his own analogy: "When you open a bottle of fizzy water, it bubbles up as it equilibrates with the air – something similar happens in the ocean."

But why will you not be finding olivine sand tucked in the most unexpected places in your luggage, clothes, and car seats for weeks after a holiday on the Florida Keys? This carbon removal method is still in its early stages. After running two very small-scale field trials in bays in the Dominican Republic and New York State, Project Vesta has recently started its next slightly more sizable project on the U. S. East Coast in North Carolina in May 2024.

A documentary on Vesta's website offers a glimpse into these trials: Flip-flop-wearing employees in bikinis, board shorts, and snor-

---

* The analogy is slightly flawed because, unlike the sponge, the oceans actually have more space for CO_2. They are just unable to absorb it because they are in equilibrium with the atmosphere. The CO_2 in the ocean has to react to form bicarbonate to make the space available again.

keling gear collect soil samples by hand in the Caribbean, then analyze them under the shade of palm trees. The next scenes show a villa-turned-laboratory where they conduct further analyses of the sandy soil samples. It might look like a dream job, but it also highlights how far we are from any commercial application.

"That is not necessarily a bad thing," says Dr. Sonja Geilert, who researches ocean alkalinity enhancement at Utrecht University in the Netherlands. "We actually know a lot less than we might think." For instance, we do not yet fully understand how differences in seawater chemistry across various regions might affect rock dissolution and in turn alkalinity release, or how the ocean creates space to absorb new CO_2 from the air. Early evidence suggests this process does not happen uniformly – factors like biota, differences in the sediment, ocean currents, and other conditions play significant roles.

As with enhanced weathering, measuring carbon removal reliably is a challenge here. If it is already tough to measure weathering on a hectare of land, imagine the difficulty in an ocean billions of times larger.

Especially if the application is not limited to coastal areas. There are also plans to distribute alkaline rocks like limestone by ship out in the open sea. The advantage? You can spread a lot of material quickly. The downside? In deep water, the material sinks fast in the water column of the ocean and loses its ability to form bicarbonates at depths of 50 to 200 meters (165 to 655 feet). "So you either need to grind the material very finely to avoid quick sinking or select material that dissolves relatively fast," explains Geilert. Less reactive rocks, like those containing olivine, are better suited to Project Vesta's coastal approach.

Using ships, however, brings a different set of logistical challenges. Mining or sourcing the minerals, crushing them to the right size, and then transporting them to a suitable beach is already complex enough. Add to that the emissions from loading and unloading ships, and you need to carefully consider the economic and environmental feasibility – hence the importance of Life Cycle Assessment. After all, most of today's mining and industrial grinding machinery still runs on fossil fuels, and global shipping is responsible for almost 3 percent of global CO_2 emissions – not to mention other pollutants.

The sheer scale of the oceans presents both a challenge and an opportunity for carbon removal pioneers. Unlike land-based methods, there is less risk of ocean alkalinity competing for space – no one's going to be fighting over underwater real estate. While reforestation, regenerative agriculture, and biomass-based carbon removal might jostle for land, the ocean is a wide-open playing field. Antonius Gagern sticks with his nautical imagery here: "Given the challenges, abandoning ship is not an option. The potential is simply too great, and we know the basic process works."

But what if there were a way to achieve the same alkalization process without the logistical headaches? Enter electrochemistry – the science behind how your phone or laptop battery charges and discharges. The concept is straightforward: When the battery is discharged through use, chemical energy is converted into electrical energy; when the battery is recharged, the reverse reaction occurs: Electrical energy is chemically stored.

A similar interaction occurs with this carbon removal technology: Seawater is drawn in and split into an acid and a base, powered by renewable energy. The acid stays on land, while the base is returned to the sea, leading to alkalization. Without the need for alkaline rock particles, CO_2 reacts to form bicarbonate – the sponge is squeezed out and new CO_2 from the atmosphere can be absorbed by the ocean.

Like Project Vesta, this technology is still in its infancy. Instead of beachwear, you will find startup employees in lab coats, standing in front of various test rigs. Their main challenges? The technology still requires too much energy, making the current cost of removing a ton of CO_2 from the atmosphere (around 1,100 to 1,750 USD) prohibitively expensive. Plus, they have not quite figured out how to safely dispose of the acid by-product on land. With so many unanswered questions, it is hard to pin down future cost estimates – current studies suggest a wide range, from 25 to 175 USD per ton of CO_2.

These uncertainties are not surprising: "The ocean community has been primarily focused on protecting the ocean from pollution and destruction. Climate was a very small part of the conversation and funding. Thus, there has been little room for considerations of and studies on oceanic carbon removal," says Frances Wang, who leads the CDR program at the Quadrature Climate Foundation with experience in field-building for marine CDR methods.

Back to Project Vesta and their plans to spread green olivine sand on beaches. In November 2022, their pilot project along the U. S. East Coast hit a bump in the road: public skepticism. Some residents of Duck, a small coastal town where the olivine was set to be spread, raised their concerns at a public hearing. With 330 miles of North Carolina coastline – 120 of which are uninhabited – why, they asked, did the project have to happen on *their* beach?

There were good reasons behind the decision to launch the project, not least because of the existing research infrastructure provided by the U. S. Army, which was co-funding it. "A few outspoken residents were not supportive of the project," recounts Dr. Grace Andrews, who served as Vesta's Chief Scientist from 2021 to 2024 and has since founded Hourglass, a nonprofit organization looking to become the trusted source for OAE field data.

What she and her team at Vesta experienced is also known as "Not In My Backyard," or NIMBYism for short. You have probably heard of it – people are generally in favor of projects that benefit society, like wind turbines or schools, until those projects are planned for their neighborhood. No one wants school noise right next door.

This becomes even more critical when implementing climate solutions like ocean alkalinity enhancement in the Global South – regions that have contributed the least to climate change but are already bearing the brunt of its impacts. Engaging local communities from the start is essential (we'll dive deeper into this in Chapter 8). This is especially true for coasts and oceans, where people often have a deep personal connection or depend on them for their livelihoods, like fishing. Gagern puts it simply: "This is absolutely crucial, particularly when we think about the sheer volume of material that needs to be extracted and transported. It is likely that the Global South offers the most cost-effective solution, but we must ensure that climate actions like alkalinization do not end up being imposed at the expense of people and nature."

In the end, Vesta managed to win over the local community in North Carolina. In August 2024, the company deposited 8,200 tons of olivine sand about 500 meters (1,640 feet) off the coast of Duck, with a projected 5,000 tons of CO_2 to be removed. A press release even shows a barge carrying a large pile of the white sand.

"Overall, things went well because we used tried and tested rules of community engagement: Come early and keep going back," says Grace Andrews. "The first time I was in Duck was a year before we even submitted a permitting proposal. In another field trial, I will soon give an update to the local community two years after it has ended."

While Project Vesta's progress is encouraging, open questions remain about how alkalinization might impact local ecosystems. "If too much material is applied in the wrong place, there is a risk of local oversaturation with alkalinity. In the worst case, this could backfire and actually lead to more CO_2 being released into the atmosphere," explains researcher Geilert from Utrecht University. Gagern agrees but believes the risk is manageable: "This is why we need to test, test, and test again."

One clear benefit of raising ocean pH levels is that it can combat ocean acidification, which is vital for the survival of coral reefs. But other effects of alkalinization are less predictable. For instance, rocks used in the process contain elements like magnesium and iron that could act as fertilizers, or, on the flip side, they could release heavy metals. "This is one of the main questions we need to answer in the 2020s, so that we know if and how to move forward in the future," believes Sonja Geilert.

To prevent reckless dumping of materials into the ocean, the London Protocol was established in 1996 to regulate marine pollution. This global agreement sets out what can and cannot be dumped at sea, and under which conditions. For good reason, the list of approved materials is rather short. It looks like ocean alkalinization may also fall under the protocol's jurisdiction, but it is still unclear whether countries will be allowed to authorize the dumping of alkaline rock into their territorial waters. This is a challenge for research activities, too, as Geilert points out.

The issue highlights that, in addition to a number of scientific questions and technical challenges, there is still a lot of legal work to be done before ocean alkalinity enhancement can be implemented on a large scale. Yet, the potential of this method is too big to ignore. "Having seen a lot of data, I feel encouraged with regards to the two key metrics of OAE, safety and efficacy," Grace Andrews concludes. "If planned responsibly, we could consider slowly scaling up field trials." Nonprofit organizations like the Carbon to Sea Initiative and Hourglass have a key role to play in making sure this happens sensibly. Before jumping into any large investments in this carbon removal method, companies should conduct thorough assessments and be mindful of the associated risks. At the same time, early support of this approach offers a tremendous impact opportunity.

Biochar Carbon Removal

On December 20, 2018, viewers of *Tagesthemen*, Germany's most popular evening news show, were in for a unique broadcast – a departure from the familiar comfort of the TV studio in Hamburg to a setting 1,000 meters (3,280 feet) underground, where interviews were conducted and segments announced. At the center of it all was Ingo Zamperoni. Typically neatly dressed in tailored blue suits, the *Tagesthemen* host was barely recognizable that evening, donning a white boiler suit, a scarf, helmet, and goggles. His outfit was not the result of a fashion faux pas but rather a necessity dictated by the unusual location. Zamperoni and his crew were broadcasting from the Prosper Haniel colliery near Bottrop in North Rhine-Westphalia, the last active coal mine in the Ruhr area and indeed, all of Germany.

This special broadcast marked the imminent flooding of the mine, symbolizing the end of subsidized coal mining in Germany, a decision made by the government eleven years earlier in 2007. Without these subsidies, coal mining had already long ceased to be economically viable – cheaper alternatives were readily available from places like Poland or Colombia. The end was foreseeable, yet the flooding represented a significant milestone in German industrial history. Few industries have left such an indelible mark on the people and the region as coal in the Ruhr area.

This historical significance was the reason for Zamperoni's descent to 1,000 meters (3,280 feet) underground, but that was not deep enough for the full story. After the introduction, Zamperoni and the colliery's employees boarded the "Dieselkatze" – a screeching, ear-splitting contraption that is part roller coaster, part suspension railway. The ride took them to the last active mining site, where Zamperoni squeezed through a narrow tube deep into the rock – no cameras allowed, as he explained before disappearing from view – only to reemerge minutes later, coal dust on his cheek and a broad smile on his face. Proudly, he held up an object the size of a brick: "This is a souvenir of real rarity value – hand-mined, one of the last pieces of coal from a German mine."

Although December 2018 marked the end of coal mining in Germany, coal remains a hot topic in the Ruhr region – not just among the climate activists fighting against lignite mining in the adjacent forests. About 100 kilometers (62 miles) east of the colliery, in the small town of Lippstadt, coal has taken on a different role. Instead of a white boiler suit, Fabian Stremming, an Energy Manager at thyssenkrupp rothe erde, sports blue jeans, a shirt, horn-rimmed glasses, and a well-groomed three-day stubble beard. Only his thick safety boots suggest we are not in a trendy Berlin co-working space but at an industrial site in rural Germany. Stremming's company, a subsidiary of global industrial giant thyssenkrupp, manufactures slewing bearings and ball bearings for wind turbines at its Lippstadt plant.

The site employs 1,250 people, 1,000 of whom work shifts involving significant physical labor. As Energy Manager, Stremming is responsible for keeping their showers and workrooms at the right temperature. "For a long time, we relied solely on natural gas for this," says the environmental engineer, fully aware of the CO_2 emissions involved. At the same time, the plant generated considerable waste wood from transport pallets. "On a business trip to Scandinavia for our wind power business, our Chief Operating Officer, then saw a pyrolysis plant in operation for the first time and came up with the idea for the project: The Lippstadt plant should have one too." The project kicked off in 2021, with Stremming taking the lead – a role well-suited to him given his previous experience in building and operating renewable energy plants.

Pyrolysis itself is not new – aware of its agronomic benefits, people in the Amazon have been using it for centuries. Biomass, like waste wood, is heated to high temperatures in the absence of oxygen, locking in some of the CO_2 absorbed by the plants through photosynthesis instead of releasing it into the atmosphere as it would if simply burned. The result? Biochar, which looks a lot like the briquettes you would buy for a barbecue.

But what really piqued Stremming's interest was not the biochar – it was the heat generated during the pyrolysis process. The goal was to say goodbye to natural gas and its associated emissions.

Two years later, Stremming proudly leads us through one of the plant's large halls. At the entrance, four large containers, each with a capacity of 30 cubic meters (1,060 cubic feet) of biomass, await. "Every day, we receive one of these containers full of wood chips – both from our own waste wood and other wood waste from a local sawmill," Stremming explains. Once it arrives, the biomass is transported through a sluice into the heart of the plant: the 3-meter long reactor, which heats up to 500 to 700 degrees Celsius (930 to 1,290 degrees Fahrenheit).

"Even though the pyrolysis process is simple in concept, these are high-tech systems," Stremming points out, gesturing to the various pipes leading out of the reactor. The most important, for him, are the ones transporting the heat generated during pyrolysis for further use.

In another part of the hall, a row of large white plastic bags, some filled, some empty, lines the floor. This is where the other product of pyrolysis – biochar – is packaged. More than ten of these bags, each about 2 meters (6 feet) high and weighing 300 kilograms (660 pounds), already surround us. They bear the logo of another European pioneer in carbon removal using biochar: Novocarbo. The Hamburg-based company handles everything that happens to the biochar after it has been pyrolyzed in Lippstadt. "The CO_2-removing effect of biochar depends on the right applications," explains Cimberley Gross, Novocarbo's Carbon Removal Manager, who is responsible for accurately calculating and selling the carbon removal credits realized through biochar.

Just like barbecue charcoal, biochar could simply be re-burned, but doing so would negate the carbon removal effect, as the carbon locked in the biochar would be released back into the atmosphere. On the other hand, when added to agricultural soils – a practice that has been used in the Amazon for centuries and confirmed by recent studies – biochar offers multiple benefits. Its sponge-like surface binds water and nutrients, making them more available to plants.

This reduces the need for artificial fertilizers, which are often produced from fossil fuels, thereby avoiding additional emissions. In tropical regions, biochar has also been shown to significantly improve crop yields.

Given these advantages, it is no surprise that Novocarbo's most common application for biochar is in agriculture. However, Gross emphasizes that other potential use cases exist: "Biochar can replace cement in concrete, substituting cement by 20 up to 30 percent and binding the carbon in biochar for the long term."

In 2022, a third application unexpectedly arose at the Lippstadt site due to unfortunate circumstances. On May 20, a tornado tore through the town and neighboring Paderborn, leaving destruction in its wake. What Europeans are typically only used to seeing in news reports from the Southern U. S. or the Caribbean, was suddenly happening close to home: Mobile phone videos captured the tornado ripping off roofs and overturning garages. Once the storm passed, the extent of the damage became clear: Not only were buildings and cars destroyed, but trees were uprooted everywhere.

While roofers worked overtime to repair the damage in the weeks and months that followed, the city also realized that new trees needed to be planted. This is where biochar comes in – it can filter pollutants and other unwanted substances from rainwater by applying it to soils. Plans are underway to use the biochar produced in Lippstadt to help the new local trees take root.

For our purposes, however, we are less interested in these side effects than in how much CO_2 biochar can keep out of the atmosphere and for how long. This is where the complexity begins: Not all biochar is created equal. The climate impact depends on the type of biomass used, the temperature it is heated to, the technology employed, and how the biochar is ultimately used.

The key factor is the division of carbon in the biochar into two pools: labile and stable. Essentially, the higher the stable fraction, the more durably CO_2 is stored. While both parts of biochar decompose over time, recent studies suggest that carbon in the stable fraction can be stored for over 1,000 years. However, this remains an area of ongoing research, with implications for the third product of pyrolysis: its ability to remove CO_2 from the atmosphere.

For every ton of biochar produced, between 2 and 3 tons of CO_2 are removed from the atmosphere. This "sink" performance is of particular interest to Novocarbo's Cimberley Gross. Once a week, a truck picks up between 30 and 60 bags of biochar in Lippstadt and transports them to Scandinavia and Switzerland, where they are spread on farmers' fields or used in urban greening projects – the latter may soon include planting trees locally in Lippstadt. Gross and her colleagues at Novocarbo monitor the process closely.

After all, it is not just about ensuring that the biochar reaches its intended destination. In a Life Cycle Assessment, all emissions associated with production and transport must be subtracted from the carbon removal performance – and here, it makes a difference whether the biochar stays in Lippstadt or is transported by truck to northern Norway. "The distance influences transport emissions and therefore the number of carbon credits generated," Gross explains.

Once everything is accounted for, carbon removal credits can be issued after a validation period. Some of these will go to Fabian Stremming and thyssenkrupp rothe erde, while the rest will be offered by Novocarbo on the voluntary carbon market.

Currently, credits from carbon removal by biochar – also known as biochar carbon removal (BCR) – are available at a wide range of prices: between 65 and 550 USD per ton of CO_2 removed, with the majority of higher quality credits going at 130 to 200 USD. This vast price range reflects the diversity of production processes and locations. In Europe and North America, the technology tends to be high-tech, while simpler systems are more common in the Global South.

Take the Kon-Tiki kiln, for example. While its name might evoke images of tropical bars and rum cocktails, its cylindrical shape is about the only connection to a martini glass. Here, there is no stirring or shaking – the biomass is burned openly, with only the flame preventing oxygen from entering, creating the conditions for pyrolysis. However, this method is much less efficient than high-tech systems and less flexible in terms of the biomass that can be used. While Kon-Tiki plants require less capital to set up and are often located in rural areas, they generally produce a less consistent quality of biochar – and even run the risk of methane release, potentially leading to net positive emissions and negating any carbon removal.

There are alternatives, however, even for the decentralized pools of excess biomass often found in the Global South. "The issue is less about the technology and more about the logistics," says Vidyut Mohan, co-founder of India-based biochar startup Takachar. "Moving biomass around is just impractical and expensive." Mohan knows what he is talking about. Before founding Takachar, he wrote his Master's thesis on this very topic: Despite the technology being available, why is so much biomass left unused?

It is not just a matter of wasting biomass and its captured biogenic CO_2 through decomposition. In India, much of it is actually burned – whether it is crop stubble on farms or waste from crop processing. When you think about the thick smog that blankets Indian megacities like Mumbai or Delhi, your mind might jump to heavy industry and cars as culprits. But here is the reality: By 2035, open biomass burning is projected to become the biggest contributor to air pollution in India, and with it comes a host of negative health impacts.

This is why Mohan and other CDR entrepreneurs in the Global South see biochar as more than just a tool for removing CO_2 from the atmosphere. "It provides adaptation benefits for the populations most directly affected," Mohan explains. "Farmers are already facing more heatwaves and droughts because of climate change; the biochar itself, as well as the revenue from its sale and the carbon credits, help make them more resilient." For Takachar, this means using low-cost, mobile pyrolysis units that any farmer can put behind their tractor. "By allowing it to move from farm to farm, we are making the ability to turn biomass into value accessible to more farmers."

With advanced technology readily available from several suppliers, it is surprising that the total number of pyrolysis plants in Europe is expected to be only 220 by the end of 2024; global numbers are hard to come by. Gross and Stremming see two main reasons for this: Even though the technology itself raises few questions, a biochar project is still very complex. "You need a reliable source of biomass, a suitable use for the heat, and a plan for what happens with the biochar afterwards," Stremming explains. The Lippstadt project is fortunate because some of the biomass is sourced locally and the heat is used directly on site. "The use of heat, in particular, often involves integrating into local heating networks, which makes the already complex planning and approval process even longer," adds Gross. In Lippstadt, it took about two years from the initial idea to commissioning.

Mohan believes that projects in the Global South are less complex, which helps speed up adoption. "Costs are lower, so we do not need to rely on other streams of revenue beyond the CDR credits and selling the physical biochar product. In our geographies, it is so hot that there is no market for the extra heat produced in the process anyway," he says.

As for the use of biochar, Stremming and Gross would prefer not to rely on tornadoes to avoid long transport routes to Scandinavia or Switzerland. But at the moment, alternatives are few: "Biochar is still a premium product with markets in Scandinavia or Switzerland, where its use is subsidized by the government," Gross says. The company is working hard to find alternative, local industrial uses, such as replacing cement, that are closer to the pyrolysis site and do not involve long transport distances. "Selling biochar to farmers is tough," Mohan admits, "whether it is in India or in places like the U. S. and Canada, where we also operate. It takes a lot of education."

Even if solutions to these challenges are found, one major obstacle remains to scale up the biochar economy: There is only a limited amount of residual biomass suitable for pyrolysis – and this biomass is also in high demand for other applications, such as bio-based plastics or biogas production. Stremming knows this all too well: "After the war in Ukraine and the energy crisis, wood market prices suddenly skyrocketed in 2022. This made it difficult for us to source the external part of the biomass at acceptable prices. And without that biomass, we cannot run the plant at full capacity."

Despite these challenges, biochar remains one of the most promising methods for achieving significant carbon removal and long-term storage in the short to medium term. It already accounts for the vast majority of the carbon removal credits with long-term storage issued quarter by quarter. Depending on its application, biochar also offers a range of additional benefits and emission reductions.

For Those in a Hurry

	Enhanced Weathering	Ocean Alkalinity Enhancement	Biochar Carbon Removal
Carbon removal and storage mechanism	Atmospheric CO_2 in rain and agricultural soils reacts with alkaline material; storage as (bi)carbonate in the ocean	Alkalinization of the oceans by application of alkaline material or electrochemistry; carbon removal by equilibration of the ocean with the atmosphere; storage as (bi)carbonate in the ocean	Pyrolysis of sustainable biomass; CO_2 storage in biochar; use on agricultural land, in building materials, etc.
Price per ton of CO_2 removed	today: 250–450 USD prospectively: 80–275 USD	today: 800–1,750 USD prospectively: 25–175 USD	65–550 USD
Advantages	Very high durability; scalability; agricultural co-benefits	Very high durability; scalability; ocean deacidification	High durability; scalable today; biochar and heat or electricity as products; agricultural co-benefits
Challenges	Verifiability of carbon removal; uncertainty regarding potential negative effects of the application of the material	Verifiability of carbon removal; uncertainty regarding potential negative effects of (local) alkalization	Scalability dependent on available volumes of sustainable biomass; complex project development; quality differences dependent on pyrolysis process

CHAPTER 6
ENGINEERED SOLUTIONS FROM BIOENERGY TO CO_2 SCRUBBERS

> "People underestimate how quickly technology can scale. If you look at the solar industry, it has grown tenfold every ten years. If we can achieve something similar, we can realize gigatons by 2050."
>
> Jan Wurzbacher, Climeworks co-founder

Given the staggering amount of CO_2 we need to remove, it is clear that relying on natural processes alone will not cut it. We need some technological backup! Thankfully, we already have methods that can boost our ability to pull carbon out of the air.

Take bioenergy, for example. Right now, we burn biomass to generate electricity, heat, or to fuel industrial processes (think of waste incineration). The problem? The CO_2 from these processes just goes straight into the atmosphere, no questions asked. But would it not make way more sense to catch that CO_2 right at the smokestack? This process is called "bioenergy with carbon capture and storage" (BECCS).

Now, while biomass has its limits, our need for negative emissions does not. So, alongside BECCS, we also need methods to capture CO_2 straight from the air – enter direct air carbon capture and storage (DACCS). This approach skips the middleman and grabs CO_2 directly from the atmosphere.

But once we have captured all that CO_2, the pressing question is: Where does it go? To have a long-term benefit for the climate, we need to make sure it stays out of the atmosphere for good. This is where long-term storage solutions come in – whether it is burying the CO_2 underground, on land or under the sea, or locking it into materials that last, like concrete.

> **In this chapter, we'll explore:**
>
> - the engineered solutions available for capturing and storing CO_2,
> - the pros and cons of capturing CO_2 from smokestacks versus directly from the air,
> - the options and potential for long-term CO_2 storage.

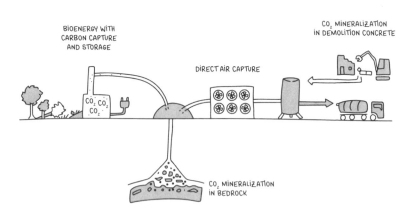

Bioenergy with Carbon Capture and Storage

At first glance, the building in the northeast of Stockholm would not turn many heads. It fits right into the city's sleek, minimalist architectural style. Shaped like an oval and covered with a facade of small brown wooden slats, its structure is somewhat reminiscent of the pieces of cardboard that are often added to packages to protect valuable items during shipping. In fact, the design is so unassuming that the architects even describe it as a "good neighbor" – an impressive feat, considering its immense size. Judging by the number of awards the building has won since its completion in 2016, it is safe to say they have succeeded. If it were sitting downtown or in a trendy business park, you might imagine hipsters working on the latest app inside.

But looks can be deceiving: It is not an office. Behind that unassuming brown facade lies a power plant – and a key player in Stockholm's ambitious plan to slash emissions. Situated in the Värtan district, the plant is owned by Stockholm Exergi, a company half-owned by the city. It provides electricity and heat to Stockholm, a city that has become a European leader in district heating.

According to *Politico*, Stockholm's 3,000-kilometer (1,865-mile) district heating network has helped the city cut its heat-related emissions by 80 percent since 1990. A major milestone came in 2020, when the last coal-fired turbine was shut down. Today, the plant relies almost entirely on biomass – bark and sawmill waste – to produce heat. It is a big win, but for the Swedes' ambitious climate goals of city-wide net zero by 2040, it is still just the beginning.

In the race toward this goal, every ton of CO_2 matters – so does every missed opportunity for carbon removal. And what an opportunity it would be when it comes to the Stockholm Exergi biomass plant. The plant currently emits 800,000 tons of CO_2 per year. But since this CO_2 comes from biomass – meaning it was initially absorbed from the atmosphere by plants – it is considered carbon neutral.

Hold on, why are we suddenly talking about a Swedish power station in a book about carbon removal? Do not worry, we'll get there.

As we have covered earlier, plants are nature's pros at sucking up CO_2. The problem? Without our intervention, they release it right back into the atmosphere when they decompose or burn. That is the short carbon cycle in a nutshell. While some processes – like biomass preservation or pyrolysis – can lock CO_2 away for longer, they require us to deliberately source and use biomass.

But what if the biomass is already being used for another purpose, like producing electricity and heat? That is the case with Stockholm Exergi. They are burning biomass, creating useful energy – but the CO_2 released in the process is just heading straight up the smokestack and back into the atmosphere. Sure, it is better than burning coal and releasing fossil CO_2; as the CO_2 from the biomass has already been absorbed by photosynthesis in the first place, the process is carbon neutral from a CO_2 accounting perspective. But we can do more. After all, when we'll need to remove massive amounts of CO_2 to meet our climate targets, a blast of biogenic CO_2 from a power station chimney is actually a gift: an opportunity to lock it away for good, thereby realizing carbon removal – on a large scale.

This brings us to bioenergy with carbon capture and storage – or BECCS, for short. This CDR method works by capturing CO_2 from the flue gases of power plants, like Stockholm Exergi's, before they can escape into the atmosphere. The plant captures CO_2 by passing the flue gas stream from the smokestack through liquid or solid substances, depending on the technology used. These react selectively with the CO_2, binding it and allowing the rest of the flue gas to escape from the stack. The liquid or substance is then treated to release the CO_2, which is now present in concentrated form, ready for long-term storage.

"There is typically about 10 percent CO_2 in such flue gases. The most common technology for separating it is to scrub the CO_2 with an aqueous solution containing an additive, usually a substance called an "amine." This technology is very well established and is the best option today," explains Professor Marco Mazzotti. He has been researching carbon capture and storage at ETH Zurich for decades and is considered a world expert in the field. He has, for example, contributed to the reports of the *Intergovernmental Panel on Climate Change (IPCC)*. Mazzotti adds: "Other approaches using solid adsorbents or membranes have some advantages, but they do not work as well on a large scale." Once the CO_2 has been captured, it then needs to be transported to a potential storage site and stored safely – more on this later in this chapter.

BECCS plays a starring role in most climate models. In fact, some scenarios from the IPCC assume we'll need 20 gigatons of BECCS by 2060 to meet our goals. To put that into context, the target for *all* carbon removal methods by 2050 is between 6 and 10 gigatons. That is a pretty hefty expectation, and not everyone is convinced we can meet it. In fact, the European Academy of Sciences recently called these assumptions "unrealistic."

However, it is important to note that BECCS often serves as a stand-in for various other carbon removal methods in climate models, simply because we have reliable data on it. While newer methods hold potential, there is still much we do not know, making BECCS the most practical option to model with for now.

Unlike some earlier-stage carbon removal methods, BECCS is already commercially available and in use. For example, the largest biomass plant with carbon capture is located in Illinois, U.S., and has been capturing and storing about a million tons of biogenic CO_2 from bioethanol production annually since 2018. And while BECCS projects specifically targeting biogenic CO_2 are limited, fossil CO_2 capture facilities offer further precedent for large-scale operations – after all, the capture technology is the same regardless of the type of CO_2.

In the UK, for example, the DRAX power station is being converted from coal to biomass, with plans to capture up to 16 million tons of CO_2 annually – massive potential but not without controversy, more on this later. Meanwhile, Denmark's wind energy giant Ørsted is working to capture 400,000 tons of CO_2 each year from two biomass-based combined heat and power plants.

Recent projections by the International Energy Agency expect nearly 50 megatons of CO_2 to be removed globally by 2030 using

BECCS. This is well below the agency's internal scenarios for the 2050 net zero target, which would require 190 megatons of BECCS by 2030.

In an attempt to keep up with these expectations, Stockholm is trying to do what it can. Alongside its biomass power plant, the city's waste incinerator will also be equipped with carbon capture technology, in order to hit the capital's net zero target by 2040. This upgrade will increase the CO_2 capture capacity to 1.5 megatons per year. However, not all of this will be biogenic CO_2, and thus realize carbon removal. After all, waste incinerators burn everything from non-recyclable plastics and residual waste to wood or that untouched spinach on your kid's plate – ring a bell? It is the latter, the biogenic part, that is relevant from a carbon removal point of view.

Jörg Solèr, meanwhile, faces a similar mission in Zurich. As Director at Entsorgung und Recycling Zurich, the city's waste management company, he is tasked with helping Zurich achieve its own net zero goal by 2040. The waste incineration plants play a critical role in this. About half of the waste they burn is fossil-based, from raw materials like oil or gas, leading to fossil CO_2 emissions. Capturing those emissions is a big step toward decarbonization.

The other half of the waste is biogenic, meaning it offers real potential for carbon removal. "It is clear that the city of Zurich needs negative emissions to meet its net zero target. All our analyses show that," Solèr says. "And we can help with that by focusing on our waste incinerators."

There are two major plants in Zurich: a sewage sludge incineration facility, which burns waste from water treatment, producing about 20,000 tons of CO_2 per year, and a municipal waste incineration plant that emits around 400,000 tons of CO_2 annually. What may sound like a simple plant upgrade is actually a huge challenge. Despite already having the infrastructure in place, Solèr faces a major investment: "Technically, it is all challenging but doable. But we are talking about investments of around 400 million Swiss francs [about 475 million USD]." Given these sums, it is hardly surprising that many BECCS plants, like those in Stockholm and Zurich, are (semi-)publicly owned.

For Jörg Solèr, clarity about what happens to the CO_2 after it is captured, where it is stored and how it is transported is crucial to the investment decision. "For large volumes, pipelines are unavoidable, but until those are in place, we need interim solutions to get started. We can not afford to wait. We have to think in stages." One such interim solution was recently tested in a project led by ETH Zurich and coordinated by Professor Mazzotti. The project transported several hundred tons of CO_2 from Switzerland to Iceland – using a combination of trucks, trains, and ships.

While many of these projects have public backing, there also are commercial ventures with serious ambitions. One example is the DRAX project in the UK. DRAX, once one of Europe's largest coal-based electricity producers (and CO_2 emitters), shifted to burning biomass and quit coal entirely in 2021. Making use of the large stream of biogenic CO_2, the company now aims to become a global BECCS leader. But the project has not been without controversy.

DRAX sources most of its biomass from wood pellets produced in North America, where it owns 18 pellet manufacturing facilities. It is here where a 2022 investigation by the BBC revealed questionable practices. DRAX had claimed they were only using scrap wood and sawmill waste for their pellets, but the journalists found evidence that primary forest wood in Canada was also being utilized. In other words, additional trees were being cut down for pellets. A practice that DRAX executives were apparently aware of, as the *Financial Times* reported in October 2024. Back in 2019, a coalition of journalists, NGOs, and watchdogs had already shown that forests in the southeastern U.S. were being cleared to make pellets, mostly for shipment to Europe and the UK.

The case highlights a common concern and criticism of scaling up BECCS as a method of carbon removal: the availability of sustainable biomass, i.e. biomass that can be demonstrated to come from sources that do not threaten existing CO_2 sinks, protected ecosystems, and local communities. As with other biomass-based processes, much of BECCS' potential rests on this issue. And the concerns appear valid. In its analysis, the European Academies Science Advisory Council estimates that global biomass availability for power plants could be up to 60 percent lower than originally projected.

In addition, despite BECCS being an established technology, there is limited empirical data, particularly over longer time periods. There is also a lack of clarity around CO_2 transport and storage solutions. "In the long term, there is sufficient storage potential, but right now, options are limited. The same goes for transport. Both are bottlenecks," explains Professor Mazzotti from ETH Zurich.

So, why the optimism around BECCS? Well, if we can tap into existing biogenic CO_2 streams – like those from waste incinerators, pulp and paper production, or existing biomass power plants with verifiably sustainable biomass – it is possible to achieve significant volumes of carbon removal relatively quickly and at attractive costs, even if these are still largely based on estimates.

Only a handful of deals have been completed so far, with only one at a known price: In March 2024, DRAX announced the sale of 25,000 tons of carbon removal at 350 USD per credit. Forecasts suggest prices could drop to 110 to 220 USD per ton, depending on plant type and proximity to CO_2 storage sites. A standout is Ørsted's Denmark plant, which secured two major deals with Microsoft: 2.76 million tons over eleven years in 2023, plus 1 million tons later. These two transactions, already the biggest in the CDR market to date, are only topped by Stockholm's "good neighbor": The BECCS plant introduced at the beginning of this chapter announced in May 2024 an agreement to deliver 3.3 million tons of CDR to – who else – Microsoft.

As evident from these landmark deals: For existing biogenic CO_2 streams, capturing and safely storing CO_2 underground is almost a no-brainer. Otherwise, all that CO_2 that plants painstakingly removed from the atmosphere using photosynthesis would be wasted. However, when new plants are built solely for BECCS, caution is needed: sustainable biomass sourcing must be the top priority. Either way, BECCS can only meet its full potential if sufficient CO_2 storage sites are developed, and large volumes of CO_2 can be transported. We'll revisit this crucial issue later in the chapter.

Direct Air Carbon Capture and Storage

The waste gas stream that Jörg Solèr deals with in the city of Zurich contains more than 12 percent CO_2. Meanwhile, the concentration of CO_2 in the air is a mere 0.04 percent. This stark difference shows just how impressive plants are at capturing CO_2 through photosynthesis – and why we should leverage their hard work. 12 percent versus 0.04 percent – in this light, how does one ever come up with the idea of filtering CO_2 out of the air?

Imagine you are on Broadway in New York City, one of the busiest, most vibrant streets in the world. You are trying to find an old college friend you have not seen in ten years. Unfortunately, neither of you thought to specify where you would meet or how to recognize each other. So now you are stuck scanning the sea of people, hoping to spot them.

Finding CO_2 in the atmosphere is a bit like that. It is not easy to identify the greenhouse gas that is having such a catastrophic effect on the planet; CO_2 makes up just one in every 2,500 molecules in the air. Translate this to your situation on Broadway: 2,499 people around you are the wrong ones. A daunting task, right? You would have to be a little crazy to take it on.

Enter Christoph Gebald and Jan Wurzbacher, two Germans who were exactly that kind of crazy. In fact, it was Wurzbacher who coined the Broadway analogy. When the two met as young students at the Swiss Federal Institute of Technology (ETH) in Zurich in 2003, no one could have predicted the groundbreaking solution they would eventually come up with. But one thing was clear: "We both had a dream of starting a company," Wurzbacher said in an interview with podcaster Guy Raz. So, in 2007, the two mechanical engineering students not only became friends but also began researching how to remove CO_2 from the air.

At the time, the idea was not exactly popular. "Back then, prestigious groups like the American Physical Society argued that it was cheaper to capture CO_2 from exhaust gases rather than from the air," co-founder Gebald explained in a podcast. "Climate research had not yet reached the point where it was possible to recommend dropping the word 'or' and using only the word 'and'." Today, it is clear: We need every tool in the box to reduce CO_2 concentrations in the atmosphere – not just a few select methods.

16 years later, there is no getting around the two of them and what they have built in the field of carbon removal. Their company, Climeworks, has become the flagship of the budding CDR industry. Not only were they one of the first to try to commercialize carbon removal, but they are also number one in many other ways: Climeworks has raised over 810 million USD – more than any other CDR startup in the world. They are also ahead in terms of employees: the team consists of around 500 "Climeworkers" spread over four countries. And as of October 2024, Climeworks also runs the world's largest direct air capture plant.

Enough superlatives – what exactly does Climeworks do? How do they manage to find that one person on Broadway, that one molecule among 2,499 others in the air? The keyword is direct air capture (DAC), a technology that directly captures CO_2 from the air.

There are several ways to do this. "Think of it like a giant vacuum cleaner that sucks in air, filters out the CO_2, and then releases the clean air," explains Silvan Aeschlimann, who formerly led work on

DAC at RMI, a U. S. think tank. "Traditionally, this is done either by using a surface to which the CO_2 adheres, or by introducing it into a liquid substance. There is also the straightforward option of using a filter, called a membrane, like the one in a vacuum cleaner."

Membrane solutions, which often rely on electrochemistry, are still in their early days. So far, the commercial heavy lifting is being done by the first two technologies. Climeworks uses the solid-surface method. "Put simply, we have vacuum cleaners, which we call collectors, that we use to suck in air. Inside a collector is a solid that is porous, similar to sand, and has a very large internal surface area. This has a chemical affinity for CO_2," explains Gebald. "The CO_2 just sticks to the surface. After a few hours, when all the places for the CO_2 are occupied, we heat the solid and the CO_2 is released from the material, and we suck it out of the collector."

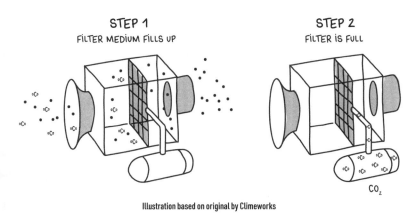

Illustration based on original by Climeworks

This chemical reaction is not new; it has been around for decades in industries such as chemical manufacturing or fertilizer production. "The real trick is making it work efficiently under all conditions, whether it is hot, cold, dry, or rainy," Gebald says. Once captured, the CO_2 could be stored or used to make products like synthetic fuels. The only way to remove it from the atmosphere durably, however, is to store it. "It is a bit like emptying your vacuum cleaner bag and storing the dust in a safe place forever," illustrates Aeschlimann.

Meanwhile, another approach – using a liquid solution – is being pioneered by Canadian company Carbon Engineering. In partnership with U. S. oil giant Occidental, they started building their DAC project STRATOS in 2022 located in the Permian Basin of Texas, with a capacity of up to half a million tons of CO_2, about 14 times larger than Climeworks' biggest plant to date. Shortly after, Occidental bought Carbon Engineering, followed by statements from their CEO Vicki Hollub that the deal would allow them to sustain their industry and continue producing oil and gas for the next 60 years.

This has raised eyebrows. Critics argue that DAC's connections to the oil and gas industry, where captured CO_2 is often used for enhanced oil recovery (EOR), are problematic. EOR is a practice in which CO_2 extracted from the atmosphere is pumped into oil fields and stored safely. So far, so good. But it opens up more oil reserves, which are then extracted, leading to more emissions. From a climate perspective, it is not exactly a winning strategy.

Beyond this, DAC companies also face a tough technical challenge: The process is energy-intensive and current technologies are still somewhat inefficient. Moving large volumes of air through machines and then releasing the CO_2 requires a lot of power. "Capturing CO_2 from the air will always cost energy – that is just physics," says Gebald. "Energy is also the main cost driver. The key is making the process as efficient as possible so we can keep the costs low at the end of the day."

Compared to the challenges of other carbon removal methods, the high energy requirements of direct air capture can be seen as a solvable task. After all, with solar, wind or geothermal energy, we have established technologies that could provide us with an abundance of renewable energy in the future.

This potential has already attracted significant investment and public support. According to the carbon removal marketplace CarbonX, DAC attracted about half of the total investment volumes in CDR in the first half of 2024. Public support for direct air capture is particularly strong in the U.S., where it's been identified as a key technology for carbon removal and is receiving substantial backing from a wide range of public funding sources. In an era of political division, DAC is a technology that both sides of the aisle can rally behind. Sensing this opportunity, Climeworks has expanded into the U.S. to tap into this support, rolling out its first projects with support from the U.S. government.

One reason for DAC's special status among investors and (U.S.) policymakers is that the approach is subject to few uncertainties. Unlike open systems such as the ocean, a DAC plant can measure how much CO_2 has been removed directly from the air, without detours via equilibrium or longer time horizons, and with the simplest of equipment.

DAC also requires less land than other solutions: The World Resource Institute calculated that, in the most conservative case, an area of almost 9,000 football pitches would be needed to remove 1 million tons of CO_2 using direct air capture. Removing the same amount through reforestation would require almost 120,000 football pitches. However, the comparison is somewhat misleading as direct air capture does not provide any additional benefits to ecosystems and biodiversity, unlike reforestation.

Of course, all of this comes with a price tag. At the moment, DAC is still very costly. For example, Climeworks charges individuals a hefty 1,500 USD to remove just 1 ton of CO_2. As of summer 2024, the average selling price for DAC is reported to be around 643 USD per ton. Climeworks, however, is optimistic that prices could drop to 100 to 250 USD per ton in the long run. Overly optimistic, according to a recent ETH Zurich paper, which suggests the lower bound price limit for Climeworks, technology in 2050 to be 280 USD. But it is Frontier – the consortium of buyers including Stripe, H&M, and Alphabet – that has set an even more ambitious target. To secure a deal with them, DAC companies need to show a realistic path to under 100 USD per ton.

That is quite the goalpost, and hitting it will require some serious modeling and innovation from DAC companies. So far, 13 early-stage DAC startups have gained support from Frontier – but now the real challenge begins: They have to prove they can deliver.

One such company made headlines in autumn 2024 when Holocene, based in Knoxville, Tennessee, announced a 10 million USD deal with Google to procure 100,000 CDR credits – at a price of 100 USD per credit. It is a milestone for the CDR industry, no doubt. However, as always, the fine print matters. The deal is loosely scheduled for "the early 2030s" and benefits from a 180 USD per ton subsidy provided by the U.S. government. So, the actual cost of production is almost certainly higher than the much-discussed 100 USD per ton target.

These high price points and the future-oriented pricing mechanisms indicate that the technology still has a long way to go until it is commercially viable. The world's largest DAC system, consisting of 72 shipping container-sized collectors developed and operated by Climeworks, is located in Iceland and will remove just 36,000 tons of CO_2 per year when fully complete. Currently, the first twelve collector containers are in operation; the plant will be completed throughout 2025. A significant achievement but still miles away from the million, if not billion, ton mark. Climeworks co-founder Wurzbacher puts the challenge into perspective: "People underestimate how quickly technology can scale. If you look at the solar industry, it has grown tenfold every ten years. If we can achieve something similar, we can realize gigatons by 2050."

"Our modules are the size of a shipping container. How many of those containers would we need to remove 1 percent of today's emissions [about 368 million tons]? About 750,000 containers. Is that a large number? Not really, it is what the port of Shanghai flips in two weeks. Of course it is a big undertaking, but at the end of the day we are building an industry the size of today's oil and gas industry."

Asked about the time horizon for this scaling, Wurzbacher replies on the podcast: "We have been running this marathon for 13 years now. At the beginning of a marathon, you should not think about the 40th kilometer, but maybe the next five. We have already covered a lot of meters, from milligrams to grams to kilograms to tons to kilotons. So we have already done some scaling." "Now the plan is to scale up by a factor of ten each iteration to a million ton plant by 2030," co-founder Christoph Gebald adds.

Right next to Mammoth stands Climeworks' earlier creation, Orca – which fittingly means "energy" in Icelandic. Capable of removing 4,000 tons of CO_2 annually, its four steel structures, each about 6 meters (20 feet) tall and 10 meters long (33 feet), resemble oversized air conditioning units. But these machines are not cooling office spaces – they are designed to help cool the entire atmosphere.

Standing under Orca's massive steel beams, it is hard not to agree with Wurzbacher: imagining what a plant capable of capturing 1 million tons of CO_2 might look like takes some serious mental gymnastics. From Orca's collectors, pipes channel the captured CO_2 to the main building, where it is prepped for long-term storage underground. Of course, capturing CO_2 is only the first step; safely locking it away for the long haul is just as crucial. This is why the technology is known as DACCS – direct air carbon capture and storage. And here in Iceland, Climeworks teams up with local partner Carbfix to ensure that captured CO_2 stays out of the atmosphere for good. More on that in a moment.

Together with a suitable storage solution, direct air capture is one of the most reliable and most scalable ways of removing CO_2. It avoids some of the issues associated with other methods, like concerns about biomass sustainability or heavy metal release. However, whether the various DAC technologies can work at the scale needed – and at an affordable cost – remains to be seen. If they can, DACCS is likely to form a significant part of CDR portfolios. It is already well suited to long-term purchase agreements because volumes can be planned and delivered on schedule.

It is therefore not surprising that some of the biggest deals in the CDR sector have been with direct air capture companies: STRATOS, the Carbon Engineering Project in Texas, has inked deals with Microsoft (500,000 tons), Airbus (400,000 tons) and Amazon (250,000 tons), while Climeworks has long-term purchase agreements with the likes of J. P. Morgan or the Boston Consulting Group. The former has agreed to buy 25,000 tons at a price of 800 USD per ton over the course of nine years.

CO_2 Storage I – Geological

Gazing to the right from Orca, the Icelandic lunar landscape unfolds before you. In the distance, gentle hills lined with brown-green vegetation rise against the horizon, an almost untouched panorama … if it were not for the white steam drifting into the sky from a series of chimneys. But do not worry, that is not CO_2. The colorless gas would be invisible anyway – what you are seeing is water vapor. These chimneys belong to Hellisheiði, Iceland's largest geothermal power plant, which helps power the nation's capital Reykjavik and keeps the lights (and heat) on during the island's harsh winters.

But a closer look at aerial photos of the area reveals smaller structures that might catch your eye – buildings that look like igloos scattered across the landscape. These igloos are attracting plenty of attention. Not just from engineers, but from global politicians, too. Canadian Prime Minister Justin Trudeau and former Swiss President Alain Berset have both been photographed here, sporting yellow safety vests and helmets. One image shows Trudeau alongside Iceland's Prime Minister, Katrin Jakobsdóttir, surrounded by pipes snaking into the ground below the igloos. It is also one of these igloos that graced the cover of *National Geographic* in November 2023.

So, why all the excitement? Because what is happening here at Carbfix is central to achieving our negative emission targets. For solutions like direct air capture or bioenergy with carbon capture and storage, it is one thing to capture CO_2 from the air, but that is only half the battle. The real victory is keeping that CO_2 out of the atmosphere for good.

This is where Carbfix, an Icelandic company, comes in. What began as a university research project has transformed into one of the world's most promising climate solutions. Iceland's unique volcanic landscape and location on the edge of two tectonic plates provide both abundant geothermal energy and something just as crucial: volcanic rock, specifically basalt, which is particularly suitable for long-term CO_2 storage.

Hellisheiði makes good use of both. Geothermal energy powers Climeworks' direct air capture units at Orca and Mammoth, and Carbfix handles the CO_2 from there. They mix the captured CO_2 with water and pump it deep underground through specially drilled holes. What happens next essentially is the same process as in enhanced weathering. The dissolved CO_2 first turns into bicarbonate. The porous structure of the rock then allows the dissolved bicarbonate to penetrate to the furthest corners of the underground, where it reacts with the abundant calcium – atmospheric CO_2 is effectively turned into stone.

Sandra Ósk Snæbjörnsdóttir, an Icelander whose doctoral thesis on the Carbfix pilot project laid the groundwork for today's technology and who was one of the first four employees of Carbfix, explains it like this: "We inject the CO_2 into reservoirs to at least 300 meters (985 feet) depth. The CO_2 is dissolved in the water, either before or during injection. By dissolving the CO_2, it loses its buoyancy and remains stored in the formation water – the second safest form of CO_2 storage. The CO_2-enriched water then reacts with the rock to form stable carbonates very quickly. We have been able to show that after two years, more than 95 percent of the CO_2 has turned to stone – that is incredibly fast by geological standards."

And you can literally *see* this transformation. In soil samples from before and after the injection, the change is visible. What was once porous rock, full of gaps reminiscent of stones washed up on the shore by the surf, now shows white deposits of calcium carbonate – the new form of CO_2.

While rock samples make for impressive visual evidence, large-scale verification requires more efficient methods. Carbfix uses a well-established approach with tracers, which are mixed with the CO_2 and injected underground. Monitoring wells are then drilled at a distance from the injection well to measure the presence of CO_2, tracers, and other elements. Proof of CO_2 storage is provided by measuring the tracers in the monitoring wells, but not to the same extent as the CO_2. "The trace gases are basically non-reactive, which means they just flow through the reservoir without doing anything. When we measure their concentration, we know how much CO_2 would be in the water if there had been no mineralization," explains Carbfix expert Snæbjörnsdóttir. From this, one can conclude that the CO_2 has mineralized along the flowpath and is safely stored.

Iceland is not the only country diving into CO_2 storage. Across Northern Europe, there is plenty of activity. Take Norway's Northern Lights project, for example. By 2025, it is set to start storing 1.5 million tons of CO_2 annually, with plans to ramp that up to 5 million tons. Similar initiatives are underway in the UK, Netherlands, and Denmark, among others. In fact, according to the International Energy Agency, projects across Europe have already announced a whooping total storage volume of 325 million tons.

But the action is not limited to Europe. In the Southern Hemisphere, Cella, a U.S. startup, is building the first CO_2 storage pilot in Kenya's Rift Valley, where an abundance of geothermal energy and basaltic bedrock create Iceland-like conditions. While Carbfix and Cella focus on mineralizing CO_2 on land, most of the current and planned projects are taking the offshore route – storing CO_2 deep beneath the seabed.

If this all sounds a bit like science fiction, it is worth noting that this type of storage is anything but new. For decades, we humans have been pulling carbon out of these geological formations in the form of oil and gas. And believe it or not, we have already gained some solid experience in putting carbon back where it came from. For instance, Norway's Sleipner project has been storing up to a million tons of CO_2 per year at a depth of about 1 kilometer (3,280 feet) since 1996 – without any major issues. Meanwhile, the U.S. and Canada are even more prolific, storing around 27 million tons of CO_2 underground every year. There is just one small catch: The vast majority of this CO_2 is used for enhanced oil recovery, a process we touched on earlier.

In these offshore storage projects, rather than the CO_2 being mineralized in volcanic rock, it is mainly the structure under the seabed that keeps the CO_2 there. The preferred storage sites are saline aquifers – sandstone structures with pores that act like a sponge and offer plenty of space for CO_2 – or empty oil and gas reservoirs. "These structures are great because they are porous, which means they have a lot of space and are permeable, so the CO_2 can move around. At the same time, they are sealed on all sides by impermeable rock, which effectively traps the CO_2," explains Jack Andreasen, a carbon management expert at global think tank Breakthrough Energy, in *The Carbon Curve* podcast. He is convinced: "Carbon storage is one of the safest climate technologies existing, mankind has stored over 300 million tons of carbon since the 1990s."

Considering the projected need for geological CO_2 storage and its growing political significance, many countries are now actively developing projects or exploring their domestic storage potential. Germany's experience, however, serves as a cautionary tale. In the early 2010s, proposed CO_2 storage projects ignited fierce public debate. Greenpeace and other environmental organizations rallied heavily against the initiatives, largely because many of these projects were being driven by large utilities seeking to capture CO_2 from coal-fired power plants. At the time, this was dubbed "green coal." The public mobilization worked. The Carbon Dioxide Storage Act has effectively banned CO_2 storage in Germany since 2012 and is only now awaiting amendment.

While attitudes have since softened in Germany, concerns remain. One key issue is that CO_2 storage will not be reserved solely for atmospheric CO_2 or biogenic CO_2 from BECCS. It will also be used for fossil CO_2 from industrial processes that cannot easily be decarbonized. What will ultimately fall into this category is still open and debated.

The role of the oil and gas industry in these projects is another hot topic. Except for Carbfix, most major storage projects in the world are led by the industry that played a major role in creating the need for storage in the first place. This has raised concerns about whether fossil CO_2 will dominate the available storage capacity. Professor Marco Mazzotti from ETH Zurich is clear: "Storage capacity is useless if it is taken up by fossil CO_2 from the oil and gas industry."

That said, complex projects in a challenging offshore environment can hardly be realized without the expertise of this industry – an ambiguity one needs to tolerate in the complex field of climate.

"At Carbfix we have a screening process for new partners. Among other things, oil and gas companies have to demonstrate robust net zero targets. So far, none of the companies in the industry have managed to show us anything like that. We simply haven't seen any convincing climate initiatives from them," says Sandra Ósk Snæbjörnsdóttir. "With all their expertise in drilling, pipelines, and gas transport, they could take CO_2 storage to the next level. Unfortunately, it is not being used for the right purpose."

Will policy makers' or public opposition to storage in selected countries leave tons of captured CO_2 without a durable home? Not likely. There is plenty of storage potential in Europe and around the world. Breakthrough Energy's Andreasen calculates that there is room to store between 10 and 20 trillion tons globally. By comparison, humans have emitted between 1.5 and 2 trillion tons so far. His motto: "If we can remove it, we can store it."

What could strand the tons of CO_2, however, is a lack of infrastructure for the large-scale transport of CO_2. Here, again, it is not just about removing CO_2, it is also about decarbonizing industry; the captured CO_2 has to somehow find its way to the storage sites. In the long term, pipelines will be the only option. "This is the only way to transport CO_2 in large quantities," explains Mazzotti. While the U.S. and Canada already boast about 8,000 kilometers (4,970 miles) of pipeline infrastructure that is or can be used for CO_2 transport, countries in Europe are still in the early planning innings. For these geographies, truck, rail or ship will be the intermediate modes of transport for the foreseeable future.

The costs of transport and storage will ultimately be reflected in the total cost of DACCS or BECCS solutions and the corresponding CO_2 credits. Similar to Climeworks in Iceland, these are services that can be purchased from companies such as Carbfix or Kenya-based Cella. Storage is currently estimated to cost between 8 USD and 30 USD per ton of CO_2, depending on on- or offshore location as well as the type of storage solution, with additional transport cost estimates ranging from 5 USD to 30 USD.

As of autumn 2024, Carbfix remains the only available option for storing CO_2 underground in Europe. Meanwhile, in the U.S. and

Canada, most existing projects are designed specifically to handle fossil emissions from industrial facilities or power plants. That said, with all but a few DACCS and BECCS projects still in development, this lack of alternative storage options is not a major roadblock – yet. The next few years will certainly be interesting, as we could see periods of either oversupply or undersupply in storage capacity across various regions.

However, this should not be a major concern for you as a buyer of carbon credits from carbon removal methods that rely on underground storage. If you do not require the credits immediately, storage providers such as Carbfix or Northern Lights with proven technology will give you the assurance that the CO_2 removed from the air on your behalf will actually stay out of the atmosphere for the long term. In essence, this ensures that the CO_2, once removed from the geological carbon cycle, is returned to it.

CO_2 Storage II – In Products

When you think of the construction industry, "clean" isn't the first word that comes to mind. Drilling, digging, demolishing, bricklaying – all bound to get dusty, muddy, and messy. And usually, so are the tools and the workers. But on a late summer morning, as we head to the yard of Zurich-based concrete recycler Spross, we are in for a surprise. Gleaming green trucks zip by one after another, their cement mixers so spotless you could almost use them as mirrors. And when we arrive at the yard, it is more of the same: Everything looks brand new, from the trucks to the bustling yard. Trucks come and go, delivering loads of concrete rubble from demolished buildings across the city. It is one of those things we rarely think about, but when a building comes down, what happens to all that concrete?

This is where concrete recyclers step in. They collect the broken concrete, crush it, clean it, and prepare it for its second life. "Most of it ends up being used in new concrete or for road construction. Recycling rates are high because it can replace valuable materials like sand and gravel," explains Dr. Johannes Tiefenthaler, co-founder of Swiss startup neustark. Tiefenthaler is not responsible for the sparkling green trucks, but he is for ensuring that the cargo is handled productively while it is in the yard.

Concrete may seem harmless enough, but it is actually one of the biggest culprits in global CO_2 emissions. Producing cement – the key ingredient in concrete – accounts for a whopping 8 percent of global emissions. The main issue? The calcination process, where the raw material, limestone, is heated to over 1,000 degrees Celsius (1,830 degrees Fahrenheit) to produce clinker, which is then ground to cement. This releases vast amounts of CO_2.

"We reverse this process, so to speak, because when the cement rock comes into contact with CO_2 again, it reacts back to limestone and absorbs CO_2. However, this happens very slowly and to a very small extent in the ambient air – it is thermodynamically limited," explains Tiefenthaler. This is why high CO_2 concentrations are used.

Here is how it works: In the Spross yard, there is a 10-meter-high (33 feet) CO_2 tank filled twice a month with fresh CO_2. This is not just any CO_2 – it is biogenic, captured at a biogas plant 120 kilometers (75 miles) away in the Swiss capital Bern, where organic waste and sewage sludge are converted into biogas. A by-product of the process is biogenic CO_2, which was originally absorbed from the air by the waste plants. Without neustark, this CO_2 would simply be released back into the atmosphere, just like what happens with biomass power plants that do not capture their emissions.

Instead, neustark collects the CO_2, liquefies it, and transports it to Zurich. There, they mix it with crushed concrete from demolished buildings. The CO_2 is absorbed and mineralizes within hours – essentially turning the concrete into stone, locking the CO_2 inside.

Once the process is complete, the shiny green trucks return to haul away the concrete for reuse.

Neustark is currently running 19 plants, with the first international site recently added in Berlin, where local biogenic CO_2 will also be stored in demolished concrete. So, it is possible that Berlin's cyclists will soon be riding on roads that literally store CO_2.

For Tiefenthaler, tackling climate change has been his driving force since his university days. "I was impressed by Climeworks, trying to 'land on the moon' by building a scalable, profitable business out of direct air capture. And they did it as a startup, not as a big corporate tanker. It is a bit like the Gauls in France surrounded by the Romans. The Roman Empire probably did not care about the Gauls, but the Gauls had to do whatever it took to survive – that is the startup mentality."

"I wanted to find my own 'Gaul' project," he says with a smile. "CO_2 mineralization in concrete is the opposite of a moon landing – it is technically simple and already makes economic sense today. That is what attracted me." After developing the technology during his PhD at ETH Zurich, he teamed up with Valentin Gutknecht, a former Climeworks employee, to launch neustark in 2019.

Neustark's innovation was not just in the technology but in the business model. Setting up one of their plants is a big investment – but the concrete recyclers usually cover this themselves. Why? Because it gives them an edge in the market. They can market their CO_2-infused concrete as having a reduced carbon footprint. Alternatively, they can let neustark take the climate benefit and share in the profits from carbon removal credits. "Our credits are high-quality because they represent proven long-term carbon removal. We then split the revenue with the recyclers," says Tiefenthaler. The climate benefit can only be claimed once: Either the concrete is labeled "CO_2-reduced," or a CDR credit is issued.

Neustark is not the only company looking to mineralize CO_2 in concrete. One of the biggest names in the space is CarbonCure, a

Halifax, Canada-based startup. Unlike neustark, CarbonCure does not work with recycled concrete but integrates its process into fresh concrete production. CO_2 is added during mixing, where it mineralizes and gets durably stored. If the CO_2 is biogenic or from the air, they can also generate removal credits.

Both companies share a key advantage: They treat CO_2 not as a waste product to be disposed of, but as a resource that improves the final product. In fact, both neustark and CarbonCure claim that adding CO_2 improves the quality of concrete. While neustark is primarily focused on CDR, CarbonCure CEO Robert Niven sees another effect as central: He told *The Guardian* that their technology reduces the amount of cement needed by cement producers by up to 5 percent, adding another layer of cost-saving potential.

This added value could be used to cross-finance the carbon removal service and offer credits at attractive prices in the long term. Today, these are still comparatively high, partly because the technologies are still new and not yet cost effective. Neustark, for example, currently sells its carbon removal service for 500 USD per ton, but Tiefenthaler believes a price of 275 USD is realistic by 2030, based on today's cost levels. CarbonCure sold at a price of almost 500 USD in April 2022.

CO_2 mineralization is just one of many ways of using CO_2 as a resource. In principle, other products can also be made on the basis of or with the help of carbon. However, a limiting factor from the point of view of carbon removal is the durability of storage. While CO_2 can be safely stored for thousands of years through mineralization, this is not necessarily the case for other products. For example, some startups are trying to produce diamonds or even vodka from CO_2 – all in the name of "drinking against the climate crisis." The issue, though, is that the only thing sticking around after that vodka is the hangover, not the CO_2.

Global sportswear company ON is also exploring how to use CO_2 as a resource in the production of their iconic sports shoes. The first prototype was unveiled at the end of 2022. Just months earlier, CEO Caspar Copetti revealed to *The Guardian* that the initial pair would come with a price tag of about 1 million USD – a hefty green premium and a great excuse for anyone whose marathon prep already comes to an end at the shoe store.

Neustark does not have these problems. But it still has a long way to go before it reaches its target of removing 1 million tons of CO_2 by 2030. This is partly because the individual plants treat relatively small amounts of CO_2. The Zurich plant, for example, mineralizes 300 tons per year. Tiefenthaler sees this as an advantage: "Concrete recycling is a very decentralized business. The recyclers usually have a radius of no more than 20 kilometers (12 miles), which fits in well with the biogas plants from which we obtain the CO_2. We scale by the number of plants, not by their size."

Today, CO_2 mineralization is one of the few carbon removal methods – alongside biochar – that can offer carbon credits with long-term storage in a timely manner. Of course, storing carbon is just one part of the story. Where it comes from matters, too. Decentralized approaches such as neustark's, which start with existing biogenic CO_2 sources and then create value from the CO_2 beyond the credit, seem to make sense here. In the future, these CO_2 streams will also gain value beyond carbon removal, e.g. for the production of synthetic fuels or products with short-lived CO_2 storage. It remains to be seen to what extent approaches to CO_2 mineralization will then be able to secure this CO_2 in large quantities.

For Those in a Hurry

	BECCS	DACCS	Geological CO_2 Storage	CO_2 Storage in Products
Carbon removal and storage mechanism	Combustion of sustainable biomass; CO_2 capture at stack; mostly geological storage	Direct CO_2 capture from atmospheric air; mostly geological storage	Onshore and offshore storage in geological formations, depleted oil and gas fields, some with mineralization	Various storage options; from a CDR perspective, mineralization, e. g. in concrete, is particularly relevant
Price per ton of CO_2 removed	today: 300–350 USD prospectively: 100–220 USD	today: 400–1,300 USD prospectively: 100–540 USD	included in costs of BECCS/DACCS stand-alone: 8–30 USD	CO_2 mineralization today: 400–500 USD prospectively: 250–300 USD
Advantages	Very high durability; easy to verify; sensible for existing biogenic CO_2 waste streams; established technology	Very high durability; easy to verify; efficient land use	Very high durability; established technology; experience with fossil CO_2 storage	For CO_2 mineralization: very durable and easy to verify; CO_2 is used as a resource
Challenges	High investment requirements; biomass must be sustainable; CO_2 transport and storage infrastructure needed	High investment and energy requirements; technology still in early days; CO_2 transport and storage infrastructure needed	High investment requirements; long project development times; role of the oil and gas industry	Scalability; sourcing of biogenic and atmospheric CO_2; if CO_2 is used without mineralization: sometimes very limited durability

PART III
FIRST STEPS

CHAPTER 7
HOW DO I GET GOING?

> "Paying someone not to emit carbon is literally paying someone to do nothing. And we know we won't solve the climate crisis by doing nothing."
>
> Microsoft

Microsoft, the American software giant, had already been grappling with sustainability long before the release of the 2018 *Intergovernmental Panel on Climate Change (IPCC)* report on the BP: 1.5-degree Celsius target. "We've been focusing on 2 degrees," said Lucas Joppa, Microsoft's then-Chief Environmental Officer. "But let's just be clear, 2 degrees is way worse than 1.5 degrees."

In an episode of Harvard University's *Climate Rising* podcast, Joppa explained how the *IPCC* report had shaken up their thinking. Half a degree of warming may sound like splitting hairs, but the IPCC made it clear: That extra 0.5 degrees makes a world of difference. Coral reefs? At the risk of being wiped out. More people would be exposed to extreme heat every year – twice as many, in fact. And for businesses like Microsoft, that means more fragile supply chains and less productive workforces.

So Joppa wondered about Microsoft's role in all this. "We've been working in this space for a long time, are we doing enough?" That's when negative emissions popped up on their radar. "We have to transition to a world where all of the emissions that humans put into the atmosphere, humans also have to take out."

Now, Microsoft isn't just any company, and Joppa knows it. They have more resources and influence than most, and with that comes a higher bar. People expect them to go beyond the usual corporate targets.

And that's exactly what they did. Microsoft became the first major company to announce not just a net zero target – but a net-negative one. They didn't just want to bring their emissions down to zero in the coming decades. No, they wanted to remove "all of the emissions that we are associated with since we were founded in 1975," says Joppa. In short, Microsoft was sending in the cleaning crew to mop up decades of pollution.

For years, Microsoft had been one of the biggest buyers of carbon credits, mostly based on carbon avoidance. But they came to realize that wasn't going to cut it. In a report, Microsoft summed up the shift in their approach perfectly: "Paying someone not to emit carbon is literally paying someone to do nothing. And we know we won't solve the climate crisis by doing nothing."

So, they went big on carbon removal. In July 2020, they called for project proposals and, from 189 submissions, selected 15 projects to remove over 1 million tons of carbon from the atmosphere. By 2023, they had purchased another 1.5 million tons of removal credits, 99 percent from nature-based solutions like reforestation. The rest was spread mainly between biochar and BECCS.

Their key requirement? Timely delivery. This ruled out more early-stage methods like DACCS, which have long lead times and are often sold-out years before operation. As of Q2 2024, Microsoft's CDR purchases amount to 8.2 million credits, accounting for 75 percent of total durable CDR transaction volume to date. Microsoft is the clear frontrunner in purchasing carbon removal credits, with no competitors in sight.

Microsoft's early foray into carbon removal wasn't just about being green; it was also a strategic move. They saw the writing on the wall: Carbon removal would play a central role in meeting climate goals. Or, as Joppa put it, "a deep belief that this was inevitable."

And if Microsoft had the resources to get a head start, why wouldn't they? By securing long-term contracts early, they were able to lock in favorable prices and build a stable supply chain for carbon credits. Even then, they saw the signs of the time.

15 years in, the market for carbon credits shifted from a buyer's market with too much supply to a seller's market with too little. Prices increased, and Microsoft predicted that the market would only get tighter, with prices set to skyrocket. So, the thinking was: Why wait? Act now.

In this chapter, we'll explore:

- why getting an early start on carbon removal can pay off,
- what options are available – even if you don't have Microsoft's deep pockets,
- the key principles to keep in mind when purchasing carbon removal credits,
- a decision framework to guide your purchasing strategy,
- who can help you navigate the process,
- how to effectively communicate your CDR strategy.

Diversifiers and Purists

Microsoft has adopted a strategy of buying carbon removal credits from a variety of methods – whether it's reforestation or BECCS. The goal is to meet their annual carbon removal targets as quickly as possible. Thus, Microsoft will not do business with companies that are not able to deliver credits in the near term.

They're not alone in this game though. Other early movers –

mostly from software and finance – have jumped on board, including Stripe, Alphabet, Shopify, and McKinsey. In 2022, these companies came together to form Frontier, a buyers' consortium that's pledging 1 billion USD for durable carbon removal credits between 2022 and 2030. Meta recently decided to leave Frontier, opting instead to source its own carbon removal deals. According to Frontier, Meta's departure will not affect existing agreements, and they remain on track to meet their goal.

Unlike Microsoft, Frontier doesn't insist that suppliers deliver credits in the near term. They're using something called an "Advanced Market Commitment" (AMC). The idea is simple: Companies agree to purchase a product in the future that doesn't exist yet. Microsoft, on the other hand, wants its suppliers to have already implemented the carbon crediting projects, or at least be able to deliver them quickly.

The inspiration for this approach comes from the creation of an AMC for a pneumococcal vaccine in low-income countries. Pneumonia was killing hundreds of thousands of children each year, but pharma companies had no financial incentive to develop a vaccine – it mainly affected poor populations. In 2007, five countries and the Bill & Melinda Gates Foundation pledged to buy the vaccine if it was developed. This commitment spurred Pfizer and other companies to develop a vaccine that has since saved around 700,000 lives – a remarkable success story.

Carbon removal faces similar hurdles: It's a new technology with uncertain demand yet offers a clear societal benefit. Frontier hopes to replicate the success of the vaccine for carbon removal. As they explain, "The goal is to send a strong demand signal to researchers, entrepreneurs, and investors that there is a growing market for these technologies."

So, what we see with Microsoft and Frontier are two distinct approaches to sourcing carbon removal credits: We call them diversifiers and purists. Microsoft is a diversifier, while Frontier is a purist. You'll find the pros and cons of each approach in the diagram ahead.

	DIVERSIFIERS	PURISTS
FOCUS	MIX OF DURABLE AND NON-DURABLE CARBON REMOVAL	ONLY DURABLE CARBON REMOVAL
EXAMPLES OF TECHNOLOGIES	ALL CDR METHODS	BIOCHAR, BECCS, DACCS
COSTS	↓	↑
DELIVERY TIME	↓	↑
TECHNOLOGICAL RISK	—	↑
REPUTATIONAL RISK	↑	↓

Diversifiers are focused on delivering carbon credits quickly and cost-effectively through a variety of approaches. They don't rule out any carbon removal methods and aren't too concerned about reputational risk – even if it means making a few mistakes along the way. Diversifiers aim to spread their risk as much as possible by working with a wide range of partners. This allows them to learn quickly through trial and error and helps them reduce technology risk by not putting all their eggs in one basket.

Purists, on the other hand, stick to one rule: Only durable carbon removal methods will do. Where exactly the line is drawn for "durable" varies from buyer to buyer. Frontier, for example, only buys credits that keep carbon out of the atmosphere for at least 1,000 years. While purists also want low prices, they understand that cutting-edge technologies often come with a hefty price tag in the early stages. They see themselves as long-term partners, willing to take on technological risk in the short run to help bring costs down over time.

Despite their differences, diversifiers and purists share some common ground: Both take a portfolio approach. Microsoft, for example, buys nature-based solutions as well as carbon credits from neustark, the Swiss company you read about in Chapter 6. Frontier, too, has invested in more than 37 different projects by 2024, including the enhanced weathering startups InPlanet and Mati or CO_2 storage company Cella – all of which we introduced in Chapters 5 and 6.

In the carbon removal space, having a portfolio is crucial. There are a wide variety of technologies, each with its pros, cons, and significant uncertainties. So, it makes sense not to bet on just one method. Later in this chapter, we'll discuss how smaller companies, that don't have the resources to dive deep into every detail of carbon removal, can still get started.

Key Principles for Making Purchases

The core principles which we recommend can be summed up in one sentence: "Start early to build a diversified, long-term portfolio that relies increasingly on durable removal methods." Let's break this down.

Why is starting early so important? Well, as independent climate expert Robert Höglund put it in our interview: "Because otherwise, there simply won't be a market when we need it."

For buyers of carbon removal credits, the temptation to wait is strong. Many companies are holding off, hoping that prices for carbon removal will drop. But if everyone waited, there wouldn't be a market for carbon removal at all.

Magnus Drewelies, CEO of the carbon platform CEEZER, sees other compelling reasons to start now: "Three- to five-year delivery is currently the best way to ensure both security of supply and fair prices." This is still possible today, but the market is changing fast. As demand increases, some companies may find themselves shut out of the market altogether or forced to pay sky-high prices. "It makes a big difference if you're a first-time buyer knocking on the door or if suppliers already know you." In uncertain times, suppliers prefer to work with companies they have an established relationship with.

Many carbon removal methods are still in their early stages. Scientific, technical, and economic uncertainties linger – some technologies carry greater risks than others. But these uncertainties affect all carbon removal methods, which is why building a portfolio of different options is crucial. "It's important to stay flexible and continuously adjust your portfolio," says CEEZER's Drewelies.

If a particular method doesn't prove to be an effective way to remove carbon, or is much more expensive than expected, having a range of options helps mitigate that risk. "With enhanced weathering, there are still significant uncertainties in measuring how much CO_2 is actually removed. We see similar issues with open systems, like the ocean," explains Maria-Elena Vorrath of the University of Hamburg.

Whether you consider yourself a diversifier or a purist, one thing is clear: Durable CDR methods offer a more reliable path forward. Many nature-based approaches – like reforestation – carry a high risk of releasing CO_2 back into the atmosphere. As wildfires are expected to become more frequent in the coming decades, durable storage solutions will become even more critical.

As discussed in Chapter 1, SBTi has issued clear guidance: Only durable carbon removal is suitable for neutralizing residual emissions. This approach, known as the "like-for-like" principle, requires that emissions from fossil fuels can only be offset by solutions that lock them away for as long as the CO_2 would remain in the atmosphere – thousands of years.

However, SBTi states that companies engaged in forestry and agriculture, for example, can also offset these emissions through nature-based approaches. This is because these emissions result from disturbing the short carbon cycle and can therefore be offset by approaches within the same cycle. Other greenhouse gases, such as methane or nitrous oxide, which are emitted from agriculture, also only remain in the atmosphere for a limited time and can be offset by shorter-term carbon removal, taking into account their sometimes greater impact on the climate. For all other companies, however, "like-for-like" means that emissions can only be offset by durable carbon removal solutions.

Finally, it's important to look beyond just carbon removal, as these methods come with both positive and negative side effects. The EU's Carbon Removals and Carbon Farming (CRCF) Certification Framework aims to ensure that carbon removal credits meet high standards, particularly in terms of avoiding harm. Although the regulatory framework for this is still in the making, it is expected to soon serve as a blueprint for many other countries, such as the U.S. However, the CRCF is not perfect, and carbon market watchdogs are particularly concerned about the inclusion of temporary carbon credits from agriculture.

For now, the risks of carbon removal are manageable, but as these technologies scale up, their social and environmental footprint will grow. Particular attention should be paid to methods that use biomass – specifically, biomass conservation, BECCS, biochar, and similar projects. As discussed in Chapters 4 and 5, projects that intervene directly in the ocean should also be approached with careful scrutiny.

Decision-Making Framework

Now that we've covered the basic principles and the two archetypes, the next question is: How do you actually put these insights into practice? There are four key steps:

"First, companies need to define how many carbon credits they actually want to buy. Then you can see what you can get for the available budget," says CEEZER's Drewelies. For companies that have committed to SBTi, a maximum of 10 percent of current emissions can be covered by durable carbon removal at the time the target is reached. "Companies should therefore consider early on how they will build a portfolio that includes sufficient carbon removal at the target date," says Drewelies.

For companies in so-called "FLAG sectors" (Forest, Land, Agriculture), slightly different rules apply. Here, carbon removal in their own value chain is also credited, even if they result from non-durable carbon removal methods. In this case, the term "insetting" is used, which was already briefly mentioned in Chapter 4.

As a second step, it is important to establish a budget, as this is the only way to build a carbon portfolio. For climate pioneers, this often means applying an internal carbon price and using the revenue to feed a budget.

Swedish financial services provider Klarna, for example, has generated an impressive 5 million USD between 2021 and 2023 through its internal carbon price. Janek Kose, who led the implementation as Head of Climate at Klarna, said in our interview, "The internal carbon price was a game changer for us. It gave us a budget each year that we could spend in the most impactful way."

Third, companies have different preferences as to whether they see themselves more as diversifiers or purists. There is no objectively correct answer as to which is the better strategy here (see following figure). While diversifiers have more options and can acquire larger quantities at a lower price, purists have the advantage of not taking any major reputational risks. "In practice, the choice often depends on the emission intensity of the financial result," says Drewelies. "Software companies with high margins and a low operational carbon footprint can become purists more quickly. Industrial companies often have to start out as diversifiers."

Fourth, it's time to put together the portfolio. What might that look like? There is no optimal portfolio, because many of the CDR approaches are continuously evolving and there are different uncertainties about important technical and economic parameters. Here we show you Microsoft's and Frontier's portfolios as positive examples.

Microsoft buys large quantities in order to achieve net zero by 2030. While projects with low durability, such as forestry projects, are still playing a role, the company plans to increase the share of removal methods with durable storage in the coming years. This will ensure that once-purchased short-term credits are later replaced by long-term storage – otherwise, past climate claims will no longer hold.

Microsoft's approach is relevant for many other companies that have already purchased credits that only remove emissions from the air in the short term. Just like the software giant from Redmond, these companies will need to make similar transitions to durable carbon removal credits in order to ensure the integrity of their climate commitments.

Frontier, on the other hand, buys in smaller quantities, but exclusively from methods with high durability. In the table below, we show an example of the approximate split between a classic diversifier like Microsoft and a purist like Frontier. The shares reflect Microsoft's reported purchases up to 2023 and Frontier's purchases up to 2024.

Diversifiers (Microsoft)	Purists (Frontier)
35% BECCS	22% DACCS
55% forest projects (afforestation, improved forest management, agroforestry)	26% enhanced weathering
8% regenerative agriculture	42% biomass conservation & BECCS
2% others (blue carbon, biochar, DACCS)	10% others (ocean alkalinity enhancement, mineralization)

We've chosen not to include portfolios based on carbon avoidance. As discussed in Chapter 2, we have significant doubts about the actual climate impact of these projects. If they don't deliver on their climate promises, the co-benefits, such as biodiversity protection, are also in question. After all, if a project doesn't truly protect the forest, it won't protect local flora and fauna either.

In our view, these projects pose a significant reputational risk for companies. Even suppliers like Klimate are distancing themselves from avoidance projects, opting instead to focus solely on carbon removal credits. "The first thing I did was to say: We don't sell avoidance credits," says Simon Bager, environmental scientist and Chief Impact Officer at the carbon removal platform Klimate, in our interview.

However, there can still be room for these approaches in your portfolio – as long as the quality is sound. Providers like Sylvera and BeZero act like rating agencies in the financial sector, assessing the quality of avoidance credits. Greater transparency in this area could help distinguish the good projects from the bad. Suppliers like CEEZER still offer these carbon credits, but with a clear long-term goal of fully moving toward carbon removal.

Climate expert Robert Höglund has provided a helpful overview of the different types of carbon credits and how they fit into different climate strategies within SBTi's framework.

Carbon credits traded on the voluntary market can be used broadly in two ways: "contribution claims" and "neutralization claims." Climate contributions – such as funding NGOs like the WWF or reducing emissions through avoided deforestation – typically can't be used to offset a company's own emissions. Only credits for durable carbon removal count toward neutralization.

However, SBTi emphasizes that "contribution claims" play a crucial role in supporting reductions beyond a company's own value chain. Many companies agree. This includes supporting restoring deforested areas or funding educational climate campaigns.

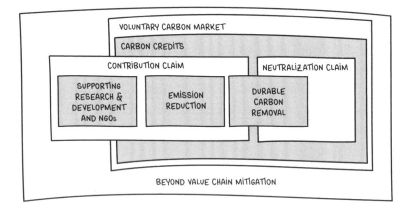

In the next step, we'll explore how you can begin your journey to net zero. There are several ways to get involved, and some willingness to experiment will always be required, as the CDR market continues to evolve.

How to Get Going

As a company, you have three main options for engaging with the CDR market. We'll walk you through each of them:

- acquiring credits via direct purchase or investing in projects,
- using platforms like CEEZER, Klimate, Watershed, or Patch,
- joining a buyers' consortium.

The first option is to set up an internal team dedicated to purchasing CDR credits or investing in CDR projects. While this approach can work for large companies like Microsoft, it's typically not feasible for most organizations due to the substantial time and resources required.

Another approach is to invest directly in CDR projects or companies. These investments can take two forms: equity and project investments. For example, Holcim, the Swiss building materials manufacturer, bought equity in the Zurich-based startup neustark. An equity investment does not mean that companies can automatically count the carbon removal toward their own targets. But they might get early access to new credits. Project investments, in turn, can often count the carbon removal from those projects toward their carbon accounting. However, as Drewelies points out, "direct investments require companies to have significant internal resources to conduct due diligence and manage the long-term risks of a direct equity stake."

The second option is to outsource the purchasing and portfolio management. In recent years, a number of companies have emerged to help with this, including platforms such as CEEZER, Klimate, Watershed, and Patch. These platforms allow you to build and optimize a CDR portfolio using their software.

They also offer pre-screening for projects. "There are so many different technologies in the CDR space," says Klimate's Simon Bager. "That's why we've developed a detailed review process. But to truly grow the market, we'll also need ambitious standards and a clear legal and policy framework."

A third option is joining a CDR buyers' consortium like Frontier. Frontier recently expanded its circle to include companies such as H&M, adding a new face to a group that originally attracted big names like Meta and Google. While Meta has since chosen to carve its own path in carbon removal, Google remains active in Frontier and also pursues additional agreements independently. One of these is with Holocene, a DAC startup already contracted by Frontier and introduced in Chapter 6.

In addition to deciding how to purchase credits, there's also the question of whether to make short-term or long-term commitments. It might be sensible for a company to start small and buy annual credits to get a feel for the market and its providers.

In general, longer-term purchase agreements make more sense. Not only do they give CDR companies greater planning and financial security, but they also help early buyers secure long-term access to the market. This security is particularly important given the growing demand for carbon removal.

Communication Is Key

In recent years, companies have often burned their fingers on climate initiatives by making statements they couldn't back up, or that later proved false. No company wants to see their name in a headline like *Bloomberg's*: "Delta and Credit Suisse claim carbon neutrality using junk carbon offsets."

The EU, for example, estimates that about half of companies' green claims are misleading. In response, the Union has decided that businesses trading within the bloc can no longer claim to be carbon neutral.

This shift is also showing up in the approach taken by providers of carbon neutral labels which are now being replaced by more carefully worded statements. Existing providers are now switching to other approaches. For example, Swiss provider South Pole now offers a "This company funds climate action" label, while the Carbon Trust has discontinued its "Carbon Neutral" label and introduced the "Carbon Footprint" label, which verifies that a brand is actively measuring and reducing a product's carbon emissions.

Drewelies says that there are also regulatory changes taking place in the EU: "Companies now have to disclose the exact composition of their offsetting portfolios in accordance with the EU's *Corporate Sustainability Reporting Directive (CSRD)*." The CSRD came into force in January 2023, and companies need to comply with the new rules from 2024. "Specifically, they have to disclose the share of carbon removal in their portfolio and the certification standards they use."

In the United States, while there is no federal law yet, California has introduced the Voluntary Carbon Market Disclosures Act, which requires companies to shed more light on the quality and credibility of the carbon credits they purchase. The goal? To boost accountability and ensure that voluntary carbon markets actually help drive real progress toward climate goals.

Both these regulations are designed to provide greater transparency and comparability between companies, and more are expected to follow. After all, many self-proclaimed climate pioneers have found themselves in trouble because of their overblown claims. For many companies, the reputational risks of being accused of greenwashing – making exaggerated or false environmental claims – are significant. And when customers sense greenwashing, it can be more damaging than making more moderate claims.

There can also be legal consequences. For instance, Delta Airlines was sued after plaintiffs argued that the airline wasn't doing anything to mitigate climate change other than buying questionable credits.

More recently, many companies are keeping quiet about their climate strategies, a trend known as "green hushing." They'd rather not talk about their efforts than risk negative press.

But for Viktoria Waldenfels, who managed carbon accounting at a German software unicorn startup, staying silent is not an option. "You can't let these scandals paralyze you," she says. What's crucial, she believes, is that companies emphasize their own efforts to reduce emissions in their communications. But she also advocates for transparency about additional measures, such as carbon removal. "It's important to focus on a long-term net zero strategy rather than short-term carbon neutrality, because 'neutrality' is a particularly misleading term."

At the same time, it's widely recognized that the path to net zero won't be easy, and many technologies and approaches are still in their infancy. "The key is to acknowledge that we don't have all the answers yet, and that we're still learning as we move toward net zero," says Waldenfels.

For companies that have already been active in the voluntary carbon market, Waldenfels sees no reason to panic. "The vast majority have stuck to certified projects," she says. That's been considered the best option in the past years. "Now, it's about communicating as transparently as possible how companies have updated their offsetting strategy and how they are moving away from talking about carbon neutrality," she explains. "The direction to net zero is clear, and that means shifting to more durable carbon removal options."

"To rebuild customer trust, transparency is now a top priority," Waldenfels adds. "Staying silent isn't the least risky strategy. Sustainability reports should address long-term climate strategies, and balancing residual emissions is a part of that."

In fact, carbon removal offers companies a wealth of options for communicating sustainability effectively. "The variety of removal methods gives companies a unique opportunity to align with their own values and priorities," Waldenfels notes. For example, a shipping company might focus on ocean-based removal methods, while an agricultural company could emphasize biochar or regenerative agriculture. "Local projects that employees and customers can see are also particularly exciting."

But that doesn't mean companies should limit themselves to such considerations. Carbon removal offers a unifying theme that resonates across all industries: innovation. "Innovation connects all companies, whether they're a medium-sized business, a large enterprise, or a software startup." It's in everyone's interest to support such a forward-looking field. As Waldenfels puts it: "Who wouldn't want to promote innovative and sustainable technologies as part of their own climate strategy?"

CHAPTER 8
SECURE, FAIR, AND AFFORDABLE CARBON REMOVAL – BEYOND THE COMPANY

> "The history of prior energy deployments is a history of injustice, poor planning, and unintended consequences. Whether this is uranium wastes on Navajo Land, deforestation in Indonesia for palm oil plantations, or toxic air in China, humanity's record is hardly spotless."
>
> Julio Friedmann, climate expert

Pulchérie Amboula lived with her family on a modest farm on the Batéké Plateau, a vast grassy expanse in the Republic of Congo. She inherited her fields from her father and uses them to grow cassava, as reported by the research portal UNEARTHED. She makes small dumplings from the flour-like root and sells them at the market. It is not a luxurious life, but she has been able to provide for her family.

Then, one day, everything changed. Pulchérie discovered a sign posted on her land: "Your field is situated within the area, Forest Neutral Congo (FNC). It has been identified and measured." Confused and alarmed, she tried to enter her fields, only to be met by men in pickup trucks who tailed her until she left.

"Since this project arrived here, we no longer work," Pulchérie shared, her voice heavy with frustration. "With grandchildren and children, how are we going to live?" The culprit behind this upheaval? Total Energies, an oil giant that is launching a carbon crediting project. To cover an area the size of more than 40,000 hectares (100,000 acres), equivalent to 75,000 American football fields, with fast-growing acacia trees.

Over the next 20 years, these trees are expected to pull millions of tons of CO_2 out of the atmosphere – on paper the project is great news for the climate. But for Pulchérie, it's a different story. "We no longer have fields, how will we pay for their schooling?" she tells UNEARTHED. "If you fall sick today, where will you get the money to get treatment? I feel like these people came to kill us on our own land."

Total Energies told UNEARTHED that it was taking concrete steps to compensate the local population. But compensation is only one piece of the puzzle. Ensuring these projects don't do more harm than good is a concern that goes beyond afforestation. It's also central to large-scale infrastructure such as DACCS and BECCS, as well as ocean-based carbon removal efforts.

The challenge of fair and equitable implementation isn't new. The environmental justice movement has long warned that marginalized communities often bear the brunt of environmental harm.

In fact, U.S. reports from as far back as the 1980s showed that the most significant predictor of whether someone lived near a toxic waste site was the color of their skin. While there's been partial progress since then, the underlying pattern remains: those who have contributed the least to environmental pollution and climate change are suffering its worst consequences.

That's why it's critical to ensure that carbon crediting projects don't exacerbate existing injustices. Ideally, they should help redress them. "A lot of the potential for carbon removal is in low- and middle-income countries," says Jan Minx, a leading researcher at the Mercator Research Institute on Global Commons and Climate Change in Berlin. As a coordinating author of the *IPCC's Sixth Assessment* report, Minx has spent years studying the opportunities and pitfalls of carbon removal. "For poorer countries, this presents huge development opportunities. But there are also risks, depending on how these projects are designed."

Because the field of carbon removal is still in its infancy, we have a unique opportunity to shape its development. "Political measures are critical here," says Sebastian Manhart, an expert on CDR policy. As the Chair of the Board of DVNE, the German CDR Association, Manhart is one of the most influential voices in the field.

"Governments need to create certainty and foster trust in these new technologies. If they don't set clear rules – and enforce them – the public will push back," Manhart warns. But there's a flip side: Over-regulation could crush innovation before it even gets off the ground. It's a balancing act.

Governments in Europe and the U. S. are already taking steps to address the safety and fairness of carbon removal. In Europe, the principle of environmental justice is embedded into the EU's "Just Transition Fund," which ensures that social justice is at the forefront of green policymaking. In the Biden administration, several top energy and environmental positions were held by leaders of the environmental justice movement, signaling that equity was taken seriously.

The growing CDR sector must do more than just pull carbon out of the air. It must ensure that the captured CO_2 is safely transported and stored. It also needs to weave equity into the fabric of these projects – whether it's sharing profits with local communities or creating local jobs. And crucially, the carbon credits generated must be affordable. Without this, the industry won't scale fast enough to make an effective contribution to tackling climate change.

This is where companies come in, not only as technology developers and project implementers, but also as major buyers of carbon removal credits. Governments, too, have a pivotal role to play. That's

SAFE   **FAIR**   **AFFORDABLE**

why in this chapter, with the finish line in sight, we'll broaden our focus to look at how a range of stakeholders, most notably governments, can ensure that carbon removal is not only effective, but also safe, fair, and affordable.

> **In this chapter, we'll explore:**
>
> - how we can make carbon removal safe,
> - how we can make carbon removal fair,
> - how we can make carbon removal affordable.

How We Can Make Carbon Removal Safe

Sule Umare still vividly recalls the day in 1986, as reported by the *Arizona Daily Star*. He thought it was raining. But when the Cameroonian herdsman stepped outside his home near Lake Nyos, he saw something strange: "I went outside and saw the moon shining." How could it be raining without a cloud in the sky? Moments later, he collapsed, unconscious.

While Sule was lying on the ground, a catastrophe unfolded. A massive fountain, 100 meters high (330 feet), erupted from the lake below. A towering wave crashed into the shore. That night, more than 1,700 people would lose their lives. Sule survived.

Unnoticed by the locals, a huge bubble of carbon dioxide had formed at the bottom of Lake Nyos. A warm layer of water near the surface had kept the gas trapped in the cooler depths – until the bubble burst, releasing a deadly cloud of CO_2 in a violent explosion. One survivor later recalled the sheer terror of trying to breathe but feeling powerless because the air simply didn't have enough oxygen.

CO_2, while non-toxic in small amounts, becomes lethal in high concentrations. If the carbon removal industry grows as expected, ensuring the safe transportation and storage of CO_2 will become a critical priority – especially for technologies like DACCS and BECCS, which capture CO_2 as a gas and store it underground. So, who will be responsible for keeping it safe?

"Safety is typically a government responsibility," explains Jan Minx of the Mercator Research Institute. "Take nuclear waste, for instance – its long-term, safe storage is handled by government agencies, like Germany's Federal Company for Radioactive Waste Disposal. With CO_2 we will need similar institutions, even though it is significantly less dangerous."

Methods such as BECCS and DACCS capture carbon in large quantities, which must then be transported. As discussed in Chapter 6, pipelines are generally the cheapest way to move CO_2. The U.S. already has the largest CO_2 infrastructure in the world, driven by its use of carbon for enhanced oil recovery – a controversial practice of injecting CO_2 into oil fields to extract even more crude, which we also discussed in Chapter 6.

However, despite having an agency to oversee pipeline safety, the U.S. system is still "terribly under-regulated," says the NGO Pipeline Safety Trust. For example, there's little distinction in how CO_2 is transported – whether in liquid or gas form – leaving much of the regulation in a gray area.

The danger of this lack of oversight became starkly apparent when a CO_2 pipeline ruptured in Mississippi in February 2020. More than 300 people were evacuated, and 45 were hospitalized. One firefighter, speaking to a local newspaper, described the surreal scene: Two people, deprived of oxygen, were "wandering around like zombies." He had to grab and put them in his fire truck to get them to safety.

In Europe, national authorities and regulations are tasked with ensuring the safe transportation and storage of CO_2. In Germany, for example, the 2012 Carbon Dioxide Storage Act regulates these activities. Among its provisions is a streamlined approval process for CO_2 pipelines, so that companies don't have to jump through hoops to get permits from every district. The law even allows for eminent domain if an agreement can't be reached with landowners – a clear signal of the urgency of developing this infrastructure.

In many cases, carbon will need to cross national borders because not all countries have suitable storage sites, or political challenges make domestic storage difficult. For example, if Switzerland wanted to store its CO_2 abroad, it would have to transport it through Germany and the Netherlands to store it in empty gas fields off the coast. The route to Iceland even requires transportation by ship. Such cross-border efforts require a robust framework of government regulation and long-term planning, but the legislation to support them is still in its infancy.

And it's not just regulation that will fall to the state – financing and operation are also likely to be state-led, at least in part. To prevent a single company from monopolizing and financially exploiting the market, a significant portion of CO_2 pipelines will likely be either state-owned or managed through public-private partnerships. This makes one thing clear: When it comes to CO_2 transport, governments will play a critical role in ensuring that it's safe, efficient, and fair.

The next challenge is to guarantee safe storage. "We need to ensure carbon storage is not just safe for humans, but also for the atmosphere," says Jan Minx. "This means storing CO_2 long-term, typically deep in geological formations."

In addition to durable storage, it is also important to ensure that there are no other negative side effects. For example, acidic CO_2 could contaminate groundwater or damage local ecosystems. In high concentrations, carbon could be lethal to animals. There's also a potential risk that storing CO_2 could trigger local earthquakes.

Several methods already exist to verify that CO_2 is being stored durably, whether in depleted oil and gas reservoirs or saline aquifers, as discussed in Chapter 6. "Geological storage needs to be verified using a variety of monitoring techniques," says Edoardo Pezzulli, founder of Sustain, a startup focused on CO_2 storage monitoring. "The behavior of CO_2 underground isn't always predictable," explains Pezzulli, who did his PhD on the subject at ETH Zurich. "But that's okay, as long as we regularly monitor critical parameters such as pressure and CO_2 movement."

Governments have an important role to play in setting clear expectations for how storage sites are developed and monitored. The EU, for example, has tasked oil and gas companies with providing about 50 megatons of storage capacity by 2030 – around 2 percent of Europe's emissions. It may not sound like much, but it's a start. While the U.S. does not currently have a similar requirement for oil and gas producers, the 45Q tax credit incentivizes carbon storage activities by providing financial credits of 85 USD per ton of durably stored fossil and 180 USD per ton of stored atmospheric CO_2.

"The key is to have strict government regulations on how often and how thoroughly monitoring is done, so that corners aren't cut to save costs," Pezzulli emphasizes. "At the same time, there needs to be flexibility in monitoring, as each storage site will benefit from a tailored approach."

In the long run, it's clear that only governments can ensure the long-term safety of CO_2 repositories. One potential solution could be to require companies to monitor storage sites for the first ten years, after which the government takes over. Compensation for any carbon leaks could be covered by a fund to which storage operators would contribute – essentially creating an insurance policy against potential damage.

Why can't companies guarantee long-term storage? Achieving net zero requires removing carbon from the atmosphere and storing it safely for thousands of years. But what happens if a company goes bankrupt, which could easily happen within that time frame? In such a case, safe storage is no longer guaranteed. This is where governments have a clear advantage. Governments, with their ability to survive for centuries and weather various crises, are often better positioned to take on this long-term responsibility.

Other carbon removal methods carry their own set of risks that also need careful monitoring. These may include heavy metal pollution from enhanced weathering or ecological impacts from ocean-based carbon removal techniques. Biochar can deplete nutrients in soils, potentially reducing agricultural productivity if not managed properly. Enhanced rock weathering may pose health risks to workers due to the inhalation of fine dust particles.

Regardless of the method used, it is critical to avoid conflicts of interest during the transport and storage process. It's important to have multiple players involved, each responsible for different aspects of the CO_2's journey from capture to storage. In the EU, for example, auditors of publicly traded companies are required to rotate every ten years to ensure that no single actor has too much influence over the process.

How We Can Make Carbon Removal Fair

Environmental problems often hit hardest those who have contributed the least to their creation. This is true for marginalized communities in industrialized countries, but it's also a global issue: The world's poorest nations are disproportionately affected by heat waves, droughts, and floods. Historically, these countries have emitted so little CO_2 that their contributions are almost invisible. For example, the average U. S. citizen emits more than seven times as much CO_2 each year as the average person in India.

This raises a crucial question: How do we ensure that the emerging carbon removal industry doesn't deepen existing structural inequalities? Take reforestation projects, for instance – if not managed carefully, they could displace local farmers, exacerbating the very injustices we're trying to avoid.

The good news is that carbon removal is still a young industry, and many of its most influential players are actively promoting environmental justice, as is the XPRIZE Foundation. The non-profit organization awards cash prizes to inventors who advance scientific and technological breakthroughs for the "benefit of humanity." In 2021, with funding from the Elon Musk Foundation, XPRIZE set up a competition focused on carbon removal, offering a 100 million USD reward to companies that can develop scalable solutions for capturing and storing CO_2. Companies competing for the 100 million USD XPRIZE must clearly outline their environmental justice strategy.

But it's not just prizes that have environmental justice on their agenda. Governments in Europe and the U. S. are increasingly tying public funding to environmental justice criteria. "I think it's great that the Department of Energy has made this a clear requirement," Manhart adds.

In addition to the procedural justice we just outlined, distributive justice is another important pillar of the discussion. This means ensuring a fair distribution of both the benefits and the burdens of CDR projects. For example, employment opportunities should be designed to benefit local communities.

Several developers of CDR projects have signed "community benefits" agreements with local people that include commitments to hire local workers. As Joe Biden's Chief Energy Advisor said during the 2023 New York Climate Week, "It's no longer good enough to have a public hearing or a community meeting and say, 'Here's our plans, this is the project' and then start the project. That just doesn't work anymore. Companies and governments need to go in before project designs are even finalized."

Julio Friedmann, Chief Scientist at Carbon Direct, a carbon accounting and management platform, reinforces this emphasis on community engagement: "I've had companies that say to me: 'Julio, this community engagement stuff is eating my lunch.' And I say, 'No, community engagement *is* your lunch.'" In our interview, he further explains how the approach has shifted: "It used to be that community engagement was equivalent to just talking to the mayor. Companies are now realizing that they need to talk to community representatives of all kinds. And that talking to them also means listening to them."

Unfortunately, this practice is still not always the case. According to the *Climatewire* newspaper, the initial consultation processes for some of the DAC hubs – funded with 3.5 billion USD from the U.S. Department of Energy – did not go as smoothly as hoped. These DACCS projects, which aim to create a broader regional CO_2 network, include players like the Swiss company Climeworks, which we introduced in Chapter 6.

On the ground, unease is growing among communities in Texas and Louisiana. "As a community, we are already last on the list," said Roishetta Ozane, an environmental activist from one of the affected neighborhoods, in an interview with *Climatewire*. "Everybody knows about this project, it was funded and everything. And now they want to come to the community when it should have been the other way around."

This situation highlights a real risk: repeating the oil industry's mistakes in community outreach. As another local activist told *Climatewire*, "That's kind of normal operating procedure down here in South Texas, to kind of organize things about 90 to 95 percent of the way completed before bringing it to the public and then asking for input." The U.S. Department of Energy had intended to prevent this by tying funding to strong community consultation processes. But clearly, there are still gaps in how this is playing out on the ground.

Europe is still in the early stages. Funding for carbon removal projects is relatively scarce, which is why many of these initiatives are popping up in the U.S. and elsewhere. Policy expert Sebastian Manhart points out that other competitive factors are also at play: "Companies pay significantly more for energy in Europe than in the U.S.," he notes. This is a major reason why energy-intensive processes like DACCS, and the companies involved, are increasingly moving to the U.S.

There's also a third type of justice, but its inclusion is still a long way off: reparative justice. The involvement of oil and gas companies in the DAC and carbon storage sectors opens the door to compensation for past damage. Imagine an oil or gas company wants to develop a geological storage site in a former oil field. They could be required to compensate local communities for the historical environmental harm they caused. The specifics would be tricky to nail down, but this approach offers the possibility of a more just future.

While these processes haven't always been perfect, reports from *Climatewire* and other sources show that these issues are getting more attention today. Taken together, these three facets of justice have the potential to significantly reduce structural inequalities. In the best-case scenario, carbon removal could empower historically marginalized communities and provide compensation for past harms. At the very least, carbon removal must ensure that it doesn't exacerbate existing inequalities.

That this risk is real is confirmed by those on the ground: "To a degree, it's inevitable that the Global North will extract value from the Global South through carbon removal. The buyers, technology, and investor capital are all based in the North," says Shantanu Agarwal, founder of Mati Carbon, an enhanced weathering company active in the Global South (introduced in Chapter 5). "We saw it with avoidance credits in the past. I just hope this time we can structure things to limit this. Ultimately, government policies can help local communities retain more value."

Pointing to the many co-benefits that come with some CDR methods, fellow Global South CDR founder Vidyut Mohan of Takachar (also in Chapter 5) adds, "From a holistic perspective, the Global South can deliver the highest return on carbon removal projects." Given the absence of local demand for CDR credits – no Indian corporate has purchased them yet, for instance – it's the positive impacts on soil health, yields, farmer income, job creation, air quality, and health that will likely drive local adoption and policy support.

But on a global level, who will ensure that companies play by the rules? Clear certification standards must be developed and enforced, because relying solely on local institutions – often too weak or vulnerable to corruption – won't cut it. The international community of states has a key role to play here, with initiatives like the EU's Carbon Removals and Carbon Farming (CRCF) Certification Framework setting the stage. "If we set the gold standard in Europe, other countries will follow," says Sebastian Manhart. That's why European regulations are so important – they have global influence and will shape the actions of major buyers in the West.

Carolin Güthenke, co-chair of the German Biochar Association, points out that regulating CDR supply chains likely won't be the sole responsibility of governments. She draws lessons from commodity markets like cobalt, lithium, and nickel: "Ultimately, governance over a sustainable supply chain comes from a mix of company requirements, independent audits, voluntary commitments, and national or supranational guidelines." In other words, there won't be a single standard, but rather a mix of voluntary measures and binding regulations.

Beyond supply chains, value creation itself must also become more equitable. It's critical that technologies from the Global North are not the only ones deployed in the Global South. Because the CDR industry is still in its early stages, we now have the opportunity to develop much of the value creation locally. BECCS technologies from India, pyrolysis plants from Brazil, direct air capture innovations from Kenya – all of these require strong local startup ecosystems, especially in the Global South.

How We Can Make Carbon Removal Affordable

If we, as a team of authors, were to fly from Zurich to London and back, atmosfair's calculator estimates we'd emit almost 1 ton of CO_2. You could offset that ton on atmosfair's website for about 27 USD, with the contributions going to projects like efficient cookstoves in Nigeria or solar energy in Senegal – avoidance projects that, as studies have repeatedly shown, have minimal climate benefits.

However, if we wanted to offset that ton with durable carbon removal, which seems like a more sensible approach, the price would be much higher. According to CDR.fyi, a platform that tracks carbon removal market transactions and prices, we'd need to dig significantly deeper into our wallets. In 2023, the average price for durable removal was still over 400 USD per ton. So while our flights might cost around 200 USD, the credit would set us back twice as much.

For CDR to become appealing to companies – and to individual customers – prices will need to drop substantially. It's hard to pinpoint the perfect price tag, but the general rule is clear: the lower, the better. A study by the consulting firm BCG suggests that once prices reach about 200 USD per ton of CO_2 removed, demand could begin to pick up. Right now, it's mostly companies with lower emissions and higher profit margins that are willing to pay the premium for carbon removal.

For more emission-intensive companies, CDR will likely become viable when prices drop below 200 USD per ton. Some companies, like the buyers' consortium Frontier, are pushing for even lower costs, with a long-term goal of 100 USD per ton.

So how do we bring the costs of CDR down? History offers some lessons. New technologies are almost always more expensive than established alternatives when they first emerge.

Take solar power, for example. In 1957, a megawatt-hour of solar power cost about 300,000 USD, enough to power the average U.S. household for a month. Today, that same megawatt-hour costs just around 45 USD.

That's more than a 99 percent reduction in the cost of solar power. In fact, solar is now one of the cheapest sources of electricity in many parts of the world. But it took about 60 years to get there – from the first commercial solar cell to a product that could finally compete with traditional power generation. But we don't have that much time for CDR.

How did solar get so cheap? As Professor Gregory Nemet of the University of Wisconsin vividly explains in his book *How Solar Energy Became Cheap*, governments played a crucial role. Not only did they fund academic research and early pilot projects, but they also helped create a market for these new technologies by supporting large-scale deployment.

Without pioneering countries, progress in emerging technologies simply won't happen. The development of solar cells, for example, was significantly boosted by early research, development, and demonstration projects funded by the U.S., Japan, and Germany.

Today, the U.S. government is once again leading the way with its direct air capture hubs, which we've covered already. "What the U.S. is doing with DAC is making catalytic investments that will dramatically accelerate technology development," says Manhart.

Governments can also support startups by improving their access to financing – through guarantees, low-interest loans, or other mechanisms. Startups typically take on the commercialization of early-stage technologies that are too risky for established industries. But these companies often struggle to access capital, especially in the climate technology sector, where development cycles are long, and investment costs are high – unlike in software, where it is a lot easier and cheaper to live by Mark Zuckerbergs (in)famous motto: "Move fast and break things."

This is where government support can make a big difference. For instance, the U. S. Department of Energy provides low-cost funding to companies involved in its direct air capture hubs, helping them navigate what's often called the "valley of death." At this stage, technologies aren't yet fully developed, and demand is still low, making it difficult for these startups to secure financing. That's where the government steps in.

But getting this kind of support is often easier said than done. In a study we conducted among European CDR startups, many founders reported that accessing government funding was a major hurdle due to overwhelming bureaucracy. Europe's patchwork of 27 states, each with its own funding pots, presents a daunting challenge for these companies. "We would have to hire at least one person just to chase down government funding, but we don't have those resources," said one founder in an interview.

The lesson here is clear: It's not just about how much funding is available, but how easily young companies can access it and how flexibly they can use it. As one founder put it, "We're asked to present long-term plans, but we often don't even know what the next year will bring."

It's a reality that rarely gets featured on *Shark Tank* or in *Forbes 30 Under 30* announcements: building a startup is tough – and in CDR, it's even tougher. "Startups should be able to focus on developing their technology; but in CDR, they also need to build the market at the same time," says Hans Westerhof, startup trainer and co-founder of remove, a nonprofit organization supporting CDR startups in Europe and India. "On top of that, their customers don't really need their product – CDR credits – yet, because the market is still voluntary."

Westerhof knows: The founders of CDR startups are banking on the demand projected by the IPCC eventually becoming reality. "Otherwise, why would they be crazy enough to start a company in this space? Until that market materializes, though, it's a matter of survival for them."

In addition to supporting research and development and providing low-interest loans, governments can also help create the markets for these new technologies. Unlike solar power, carbon removal often resembles waste management – meaning the product is not something people or businesses can use directly. The solution? Selling carbon removal credits. "The voluntary carbon market isn't enough. It's too small, too fragile. If we want to scale this up, governments have to step in," said one of the founders we interviewed.

Na'im Merchant, co-founder and Executive Director of independent policy initiative Carbon Removal Canada, is focused on scaling up carbon removal through policy. He points out the limits of the voluntary carbon market and emphasizes the need for government action: "The voluntary carbon market plays a crucial catalytic role for CDR, but its volume is currently only 2 billion USD and consists mainly of avoidance credits. In contrast, the global compliance market is worth around 800 billion USD. The endgame is compliance markets, where polluters have to pay for carbon removal."

In a compliance carbon market, companies are required to buy or receive allowances for their greenhouse gas emissions, pushing them to reduce emissions. The largest compliance market currently is the EU Emissions Trading System (EU ETS), where companies are given a limited number of carbon allowances and must trade them if they exceed or reduce their emissions, helping to cap overall emissions and encourage cleaner practices.

Integrating CDR into the EU ETS could make a huge difference, where currently, carbon removal credits are still excluded. The European Union, however, is working on a Certification Framework for carbon removal credits. "The key challenge is to ensure proper Monitoring, Reporting, and Verification of carbon removal. This needs to be the top priority," says Jan Minx. The framework will ensure that for every ton of carbon sold, there is 1 ton removed. Without this, the integration of carbon removal into the EU ETS could undermine the current pricing system.

Still, the direction of travel is clear: integrating carbon removal into a large, stable market like the EU ETS would be a "game changer," as CDR expert Robert Höglund puts it. Since this will take time, voluntary purchases of carbon removal by companies are currently driving down costs.

For Erin Burns, Executive Director at Carbon180, a U.S.-based carbon removal NGO, it seems natural and realistic for the EU to transition from voluntary to compliance markets. She notes, however, that this is less likely to happen in the U.S.: "What has always worked in the U.S. for climate action is not a single 'silver bullet' policy, but a mix of small and medium-sized policies. Here, I see federal purchasing as a great and feasible way to scale durable, highly accountable carbon removal." Na'im Merchant agrees, adding that "government action is crucial, and public procurement can act as the bridge between voluntary and compliance markets."

Government purchases of carbon removal credits can indeed be a powerful tool. In 2023, for example, the U.S. Department of Energy committed about 35 million USD to directly procure these credits, and the Canadian government committed to purchase at least 10 million CAD (7.55 million USD) in carbon removal in 2024. Both important initiatives – though celebrated more for their symbolic impact. In the long run, we'll need larger, more stable purchase volumes to really grow the market.

For Those in a Hurry

- To make carbon removal safe, affordable, and fair, we need to build an ecosystem that includes many different players.
- Governments play a central role in making this happen.
- To make carbon removal safe, long-term solutions for carbon transport and storage must be established. Governments can help by providing clear regulations, financing, and long-term risk-taking.
- To make carbon removal fair, three key aspects must be addressed: the involvement of local communities, the equitable distribution of profits, and reparative justice – making amends for past environmental damage. The oil and gas industry, for example, could be required to build carbon storage sites that also create local jobs.
- To make carbon removal affordable, we need a coalition of pioneers that includes young companies, investors, and government agencies. History shows that government action can play a vital role in increasing the supply of and demand for carbon removal, just as it did in the solar industry.

EPILOGUE

> "I am optimistic. If we get it right, everyone can benefit from carbon removal."
>
> Caitlin Wale, South African investor

You've done it – congratulations on navigating the carbon jungle! You may remember the Head of Sustainability from the preface. She wanted to know how to build a resilient, long-term climate strategy, especially when it came to handling those intractable residual emissions. So, what did we recommend?

Our advice can be boiled down to the key takeaways of this book, which we'd like to briefly remind you of here:

How to Get Going:
- For companies, the Science Based Targets initiative (SBTi) provides the best framework for getting ready for tomorrow. While SBTi isn't perfect, it is based on the latest scientific research – the same research that will guide many of the policy decisions that businesses will have to adapt to.
- Even if your company hasn't yet committed to a net zero target, it's worth thinking about carbon removal today. SBTi is likely to incentivize investing in carbon removal in the near future, and it makes sense to start early – supplies are likely

to run out quickly. Plus, early adopters have a critical role to play in scaling up the carbon removal industry, driving down prices, and increasing availability.
- Currently, the voluntary carbon market relies mainly on credits from carbon reduction or avoidance projects, such as forest conservation. However, many studies highlight significant quality issues with these projects. SBTi also points out that avoidance projects aren't suitable for meeting corporate emissions targets – unless you're in the forestry or agriculture sector.

Carbon Removal – Which Methods Can Help Us Reach the Finish Line

- SBTi allows carbon removal as part of achieving net zero, but emphasizes that most emissions should be reduced internally – typically by 90 percent. The remaining emissions can be offset by durable carbon removal.
- Matching your company's emissions with the right carbon removal method is essential – this is known as the "like-for-like" principle. In other words, the type of carbon cycle matters when offsetting emissions.
- For emissions that come from the fast carbon cycle – like those from agriculture or forestry – nature-based solutions like regenerative agriculture or ecosystem restoration are fitting options. But these options are only suitable if you're already in the agricultural or forestry business; otherwise, they can't count toward your company's climate goals.
- For emissions coming from the slow carbon cycle, such as those from burning fossil fuels, only methods that provide durable carbon removal, ideally for thousands of years, are appropriate. Given the limited availability of durable carbon removal, starting now can be a smart move.

- Methods such as biochar carbon removal, enhanced weathering, bioenergy with CCS, and direct air carbon capture with storage are good options. Ocean alkalinity enhancement can also play a role here.
- Each carbon removal method has its pros and cons: Methods that operate in the fast carbon cycle often have many co-benefits, such as enhancing biodiversity. But, by their very nature, these approaches provide only short-term carbon storage.
- On the other hand, removal methods that primarily work in the slow carbon cycle offer long-term storage but come with challenges of verification, energy requirements, and biomass availability.

The First Steps

- There are two main ways to get started with carbon removal today: You can be a diversifier like Microsoft or a purist like the buyers' consortium Frontier.
- Diversifiers mix all established carbon removal methods, whether they tap into the short-term or long-term carbon cycle. Purists, on the other hand, focus solely on methods that durably lock away carbon.
- For most companies, building their own portfolio is too time-consuming and resource-intensive. That's where platforms like CEEZER or Klimate, as well as buyers' consortia like Frontier, come in – offering a practical first step.
- There are scientific uncertainties associated with all carbon removal methods, especially those that operate in open systems such as the ocean.
- That is why it is important for companies to communicate that we are all on a journey to net zero and that there is still a lot to learn. We don't have all the answers yet, but we're moving in the right direction.

- Also, companies aren't alone in this. Governments have a key role to play in making carbon removal safe, fair, and affordable. They can help by setting clear regulations, linking subsidies to social criteria, and supporting pilot plants.
- Government purchases can also make a difference – like when the U. S. Department of Energy announced in 2023 it would provide 35 million USD to buy carbon removal credits.

A Long Road Ahead

The field of carbon removal has grown significantly over the past years. Sales of durable carbon removal increased by more than 500 percent between 2022 and 2023, and a record 4.8 million tons of CDR were purchased in the second quarter of 2024 alone, more than in all of 2023. Every carbon removal conference we've attended has been packed with enthusiastic people eager to make a difference.

Yet, despite the momentum, the growth rate of the carbon removal sector is still too slow to meet the goals of the Paris Climate Agreement. The authors of *The State of CDR* report, published in 2024, estimate that by 2030 the gap between what we need for the Paris targets and the expected CDR scale-up will be nearly 4 gigatons. As a point of reference, the current total U. S. emissions are about 5.5 gigatons per year.

This slow pace has some experts worried. There's a concern that without faster growth, many CDR startups could struggle or even go under. Right now, these startups are navigating a tough market – few buyers, difficult government funding, and various technical hurdles to overcome. With Running Tide and Nori (both covered in Chapter 4), two early darlings of the CDR market have already folded; it is likely that more will follow.

In our interview, expert Robert Höglund says: "It's entirely possible that we won't generate enough demand to kickstart the carbon removal market to the extent needed. If I had to bet, I'd say we won't get it right." Then he laughs: "Maybe I'm just a naysayer."

In contrast to Höglund, management consultancy BCG paints a much more optimistic picture in its report *The Time for Carbon Removal Has Come*, produced in collaboration with organizations active in the carbon removal space. As early as 2030, BCG predicts a huge gap between supply and demand for carbon removal. They foresee many companies entering the market, leading to significant supply shortages. According to another *BCG Report*, the global economic potential of CDR could reach up to 1 trillion USD per year by 2050 – at par with today's global airline industry.

As always, the words of statistician George Box hold true: "All models are wrong, but some are useful." None of us has a crystal ball to predict the long-term trajectory of the carbon removal market.

What is clear, however, is that there are certain levers we can pull to kickstart the carbon removal market. The science is clear: We need massive amounts of carbon removal to meet climate goals.

Outlook

The more buyers that enter the market, the greater the likelihood that a market of affordable carbon removal credits will emerge in the long term. Net zero targets are crucial here, because the need for carbon removal is implied by the very concept of "net."

However, many current net zero targets are vague and incomplete, often lacking a clear roadmap for carbon removal.

SBTi's clear guidelines can be helpful in this context. Yet, the initiative still lacks incentives for companies to act now, though this might change in the near term. An analysis by the market platform CDR.fyi shows that only one in 200 companies with an science based target is already active in the carbon removal market. These include companies such as Klarna, Airbus, and McKinsey.

More specific guidance from SBTi could make a big difference. As the founder of a European CDR startup told us: "The biggest threat to the carbon removal sector is the status quo – many big players are doing nothing." Companies can already contribute significantly to market growth by setting clear targets and buying carbon removal credits early.

Of course, scaling the market in the long run will require government support. Unfortunately, as another founder pointed out, "Government policy is too volatile to guarantee future revenues. Climate policy is highly politicized and changes could disrupt CDR's positive development."

"Our hope is to grow the CDR market to the point where governments step up and take responsibility for scaling it up," says Höglund. Integrating CDR into existing emissions trading systems, like the European Emissions Trading System, could be a game changer – but that won't happen until 2031 at the earliest, when the next trading phase begins. "And there are still many details to work out," adds policy expert Manhart, "such as ensuring that emission reductions and removals don't get lumped together. Linked but separate trading systems could help."

But government support shouldn't just focus on the demand side. Governments can also help the nascent carbon removal industry by supporting the supply side – funding scientific research, building pilot plants, and developing large-scale prototypes.

Some might think that we should just let the market solve it. However, if we do, a small group of venture capitalists will end up deciding which removal methods will succeed. As one founder put it, "The carbon credits market isn't mature enough to be attractive to anyone beyond a few VCs and niche investors."

Venture capital typically demands fast, high returns, which means that CDR methods with additional revenue streams, greater technical maturity or lower levels of uncertainty are considered more attractive. This is why so much investment is going into biochar and DACCS. By the first half of 2024, over 90 percent of carbon removal credits were delivered from biochar projects.

That's not inherently bad, but it runs the risk of turning the carbon removal sector into a monoculture. Each carbon removal method has its own scaling challenges, whether it's land, biomass, or energy availability. That is why governments, like companies, need to diversify by supporting a portfolio of carbon removal technologies. "The 2020s are the years to figure out what works, and what does not. But one thing is already certain: If we are going to meet the climate crisis in a meaningful way, we will need a mix of solutions alongside each other. One silver bullet is not going to cut it," says remove founder Hans Westerhof.

Governments can help prevent the carbon removal landscape from becoming a monoculture by actively promoting underrepresented approaches, such as ocean-based methods. For example, Germany's funding program "CDRmare" is exploring different ways to better integrate the ocean into carbon removal through a broad research consortium. More funding for Research & Development in these areas could greatly benefit the entire field of carbon removal.

These efforts show that carbon removal is not only about achieving net zero but also about promoting a diverse set of methods that ensure long-term climate resilience. As Na'im Merchant puts it, "We know net zero is just a political target, but it's not the endgame for climate change. The endgame for climate change is that we return our Earth's system to something that is actually livable for people, where ecosystems are healthy, and communities are safe."

Global Justice

It's not just the diversification of a few carbon removal approaches that we need to address. The same goes for geographic diversification, especially where areas currently not participating in the carbon removal markets have most of the natural resources required to reverse the climate crisis. "I'm very concerned that we're repeating the industrial revolution," says South African entrepreneur and investor Caitlin Wale, who spent years working at a London-based venture capital firm specializing in carbon removal. "The resources are coming from the Global South, but the profits are going to the North."

"The reason I moved back to South Africa was to make the field of carbon removal big here. We have everything we need – natural resources, plenty of land, and talent," says Wale, who founded Kinjani, a startup incubator and investor that supports African climate founders. "It's very important to me that local founders can be part of the growing carbon removal market, and also benefit from it."

In fact, much of the potential for carbon removal lies in the Global South. There's vast undeveloped land suitable for nature-based solutions, plenty of excess biomass and alkaline rock as well as abundant storage sites for CO_2.

Yet, if you look at a map of carbon removal projects, most activity is concentrated in the Global North, where most of the technology is being developed. However, there are signs of change: Startups like Cella in Kenya are gaining a foothold in carbon storage, and entrepreneurial initiatives are emerging in India and Brazil, some of which we have featured in Chapters 4 to 6.

It's hard to predict exactly how carbon removal will evolve over the coming years. But one thing is certain: We're going to need vast amounts of carbon removal – billions of tons. Every year. It's essential to ensure that the benefits of this emerging industry don't end up solely in the Global North. After all, the wealthy North bears much of the responsibility for the climate crisis, while the consequences are often felt most acutely by people in the Global South. "I am optimistic," says Wale. "If we get it right, everyone can benefit from carbon removal."

ACKNOWLEDGMENTS

We've written a lot about the great potential of carbon removal in this book, but we've also explored the technical and economic uncertainties of this young industry.

One thing, however, is certain: This book wouldn't be in your hands without the help, encouragement, and openness of many wonderful people. We'd like to take a moment to thank them from the bottom of our hearts.

First, we'd like to thank our agent Petra Hermanns, who believed in the project early on and helped us find the perfect home for our book at Campus.

We'd also like to express our sincere gratitude to our editor, Patrik Ludwig, whose practical approach and valuable advice were instrumental in making this book a reality.

A special thanks to Lorna Schütte for the beautiful illustrations. Your creativity and swift delivery were invaluable.

This book would not exist without the multitude of people who were willing to talk to us about their work on net zero and carbon removal. Your enthusiasm, energy, and openness inspired us every day to bring this project to life!

A heartfelt thank you to: Robert Höglund, Sebastian Manhart, Cyril Brunner, Carolin Güthenke, Viktoria Waldenfels, Magnus Drewelies, Jan Minx, Janek Kose, Simon Bager, Caitlin Wale, Edoardo Pezzulli, Julio Friedmann, Na'im Merchant, Hans Westerhof, Erin Burns, Jack Andreasen, Petrissa Eckle, Ivo Degn, Tom Crowther, Frauke Kracke, Cimberley Gross, Fabian Stremming,

Antonius Gagern, Maria-Elena Vorrath, Thorben Amann, Maurice Bryson, Cara Maesano, Jörg Solèr, Silvain Aeschlimann, Marco Mazzotti, Johannes Tiefenthaler, Frances Wang, Sandra Ósk Snæbjörnsdóttir, Vidyut Mohan, Max DuBuisson, Shantanu Agarwal, Radhika Moolgavkar, Sonja Geilert, Grace Andrews, Jimmy Voorhis and Volker Hoffmann.

We also want to thank everyone whose feedback shaped the title and cover of this book.

Lastly, we owe a huge debt of gratitude to all the researchers and journalists whose work on the climate crisis, net zero, and carbon removal laid the foundation for this book – thank you!

SOURCES

Unless otherwise noted, all online sources were last accessed on October 31, 2024.

Preface

Bloomberg (2022). Junk Carbon Offsets Are What Make These Big Companies Carbon Neutral. https://www.bloomberg.com/graphics/2022-carbon-offsets-renewable-energy/

Goodreads (2023). William Gibson Quotes. https://www.goodreads.com/author/quotes/9226.William_Gibson

Microsoft (2020). Microsoft will be carbon negative by 2030. https://blogs.microsoft.com/blog/2020/01/16/microsoft-will-be-carbon-negative-by-2030/

Science Based Targets (2023). Driving Ambitious Corporate Climate Action. https://sciencebasedtargets.org/

Science Based Targets (2024). SBTi Insider: August 2024. https://www.linkedin.com/pulse/sbti-insider-august-2024-science-based-targets-ycpee/?trackingId=Uv%2FrOOkORoa3XeURrlUEvQ%3D%3D

The Guardian (2023). Revealed: more than 90% of rainforest carbon offsets by biggest certifier are worthless, analysis shows. https://www.theguardian.com/environment/2023/jan/18/revealed-forest-carbon-offsets-biggest-provider-worthless-verra-aoe

Chapter 1

Business Insider (2023). The Rise and Fall of Blockbuster. https://www.businessinsider.com/rise-and-fall-of-blockbuster

Dieter Helm (2023). The Net Zero 2035 Target for Electricity is Not Credible. https://dieterhelm.co.uk/energy-climate/the-net-zero-2035-target-for-electricity-is-not-credible/

Die Zeit (2024). Greenwashing in the USA: Questionable Seal of Quality. https://www.zeit.de/wirtschaft/2024-08/greenwashing-usa-emissions-compensation-abroad-english/komplettansicht

MSCI Sustainability Institute (2024). US firms fall further behind global peers on climate disclosure. https://www.msci-institute.com/insights/us-firms-fall-further-behind-global-peers-on-climate-disclosure/

Nesta (2015). Winning Together: A Guide to Successful Corporate-Startup Collaborations. https://www.nesta.org.uk/blog/winning-together-a-guide-to-successful-corporate-startup-collaboration/

Net Zero Tracker (2022). Net Zero Stocktake Report. https://ca1-nzt.edcdn.com/Net-Zero-Tracker/Net-Zero-Stocktake-Report-2022.pdf

Net Zero Tracker (2024). https://zerotracker.net/

New York Times (2019). The World's Last Blockbuster Has No Plans to Close. https://www.nytimes.com/2019/03/06/business/last-blockbuster-store.html

PA Future (2023). Inflexibility for SMEs is latest criticism levelled at SBTi. https://future.portfolio-adviser.com/sbti-net-zero-smes/

S&P Global (2023). 22 US companies singled out for not filing science-based climate targets. https://www.spglobal.com/marketintelligence/en/news-insights/latest-news-headlines/22-us-companies-singled-out-for-not-filing-science-based-climate-targets-76869741

Science Based Targets (2024). Aligning Corporate Value Chains to Global Climate Goals. https://sciencebasedtargets.org/resources/files/Aligning-corporate-value-chains-to-global-climate-goals-SBTi-Research-Scope-3-Discussion-Paper.pdf

Science Based Targets (2024). The Net-Zero Standard. https://sciencebasedtargets.org/resources/files/Net-Zero-Standard.pdf

Science Based Targets (2024). SBTi Insider: August 2024. https://www.linkedin.com/pulse/sbti-insider-august-2024-science-based-targets-ycpee/?trackingId=Uv%2FrOOkORoa3XeURrlUEvQ%3D%3D

Science Based Targets (2024). SBTi Monitoring Report 2023. https://sciencebasedtargets.org/resources/files/SBTiMonitoringReport2023.pdf

Science Based Targets (2024). Statement from the SBTi Board of Trustees. https://sciencebasedtargets.org/news/statement-from-the-sbti-board-of-trustees-on-use-of-environmental-attribute-certificates-including-but-not-limited-to-voluntary-carbon-markets-for-abatement-purposes-limited-to-scope-3

Science Based Targets (2024). Target Dashboard. https://sciencebasedtargets.org/target-dashboard

The White House (2022). Inflation Reduction Act Guidebook. https://www.whitehouse.gov/cleanenergy/inflation-reduction-act-guidebook/

Top Agrar (2012). Photovoltaikförderung: So sinnvoll wie Ananas züchten in Alaska. https://www.topagrar.com/energie/news/grossmann-photovoltaikfoerderung-so-sinnvoll-wie-ananas-zuechten-in-alaska-9242657.html

Trellis (2024). SEC passes new emissions rule. https://trellis.net/article/sec-passes-new-emissions-rule-heres-what-you-need-know/

UK Government (2019). UK becomes first major economy to pass net zero emissions law. https://www.gov.uk/government/news/uk-becomes-first-major-economy-to-pass-net-zero-emissions-law

Vanity Fair (2019). Netflix's Crazy, Doomed Meeting With Blockbuster. https://www.vanityfair.com/news/2019/09/netflixs-crazy-doomed-meeting-with-blockbuster

Chapter 2

Bundesregierung (2022). Klimaschutzgesetz 2021. https://www.bundesregierung.de/breg-de/schwerpunkte/klimaschutz/klimaschutzgesetz2021-1913672

Calel et al. (2021). Do Carbon Offsets Offset Carbon? https://www.lse.ac.uk/granthaminstitute/publication/do-carbon-offsets-offset-carbon/

Cames et al. (2016). How additional is the Clean Development Mechanism? https://climate.ec.europa.eu/system/files/2017-04/clean_dev_mechanism_en.pdf

CarbonBetter (2022). Fierce Whiskers Launches World's First Carbon-Negative Bourbon. https://carbonbetter.com/story/carbon-negative-bourbon/

Deming Institute (2015). A Bad System Will Beat a Good Person Every Time. https://deming.org/a-bad-system-will-beat-a-good-person-every-time/

Gill-Wiehl et al. (2023). Cooking the books: Pervasive over-crediting from cookstoves offset methodologies. https://unfccc.int/sites/default/files/resource/SB008_call_for_input_annotations_Berkeley%20Carbon%20Trading%20Project_Cookstove.pdf

McKinsey & Company (2021). A Blueprint for Scaling Voluntary Carbon Markets to Meet the Climate Challenge. https://www.mckinsey.com/capabilities/sustainability/our-insights/a-blueprint-for-scaling-voluntary-carbon-markets-to-meet-the-climate-challenge

Net Zero Tracker (2024). https://zerotracker.net/

New York Times (2019). Rosie Ruiz, Who Faked Victory in Boston Marathon, Dies at 66. https://www.nytimes.com/2019/08/08/sports/rosie-ruiz-boston-marathon-dead.html

NPR (2016). Transcript Planet Money: Money Trees. https://www.npr.org/transcripts/455941812

Probst et al. (2024). Systematic assessment of the achieved emission reductions of carbon crediting projects. https://doi.org/10.17863/CAM.109495

S&P Global (2021). Voluntary carbon markets: how they work, how they're priced and who's involved. https://www.spglobal.com/commodityinsights/en/market-insights/blogs/energy-transition/061021-voluntary-carbon-markets-pricing-participants-trading-corsia-credits

Science Based Targets (2024). The Net-Zero Standard. https://sciencebasedtargets.org/resources/files/Net-Zero-Standard.pdf

Smith School of Enterprise and the Environment (2020). The Oxford Principles for Net Zero Aligned Carbon Offsetting. https://www.smithschool.ox.ac.uk/sites/default/files/2022-01/Oxford-Offsetting-Principles-2020.pdf

The Guardian (2023). BP and Spotify bought carbon credits at risk of link to forced Uyghur labour in China. https://www.theguardian.com/environment/2023/nov/13/carbon-credits-at-risk-of-link-to-uyghur-forced-labour-bought-by-bp-and-spotify

The New Yorker (2023). The Great Cash for Carbon Hustle. https://www.newyorker.com/magazine/2023/10/23/the-great-cash-for-carbon-hustle

Times Online (2007). The top 50 sporting scandals. https://www.thetimes.com/article/the-top-50-sporting-scandals-3r38g20v3hk

West et al. (2023). Action needed to make carbon offsets from forest conservation work for climate change mitigation. https://www.science.org/doi/10.1126/science.ade3535

Chapter 3

Guinness World Records (2022). Most views for a cat on YouTube. https://www.guinnessworldrecords.com/world-records/469238-most-views-for-a-cat-on-youtube

Nasa Earth Observatory (2011). The Carbon Cycle. https://earthobservatory.nasa.gov/features/CarbonCycle

Chapter 4

Amazon (2023). The World's Most Dangerous Show – Season 1 – Episode 4. https://www.amazon.de/Joko-Winterscheidt-Presents-Dangerous-Staffel/dp/B0B8JXGHL8

Arkema et al. (2023). Evidence-based target setting informs blue carbon strategies for nationally determined contributions. https://doi.org/10.1038/s41559-023-02081-1

Badgley et al. (2022). California's forest carbon offsets buffer pool is severely undercapitalized. https://www.frontiersin.org/articles/10.3389/ffgc.2022.930426

Bastin et al. (2019). The global tree restoration potential. https://doi.org/10.1126/science.aax0848

Bloomberg Law (2022). One California Forest Thinning Project Upheld, Another Rejected. https://news.bloomberglaw.com/litigation/one-california-forest-thinning-project-upheld-another-rejected

Bonnchallenge.org (2024). The Bonn Challenge. https://www.bonnchallenge.org/

Boyd et al. (2022). Potential negative effects of ocean afforestation on offshore ecosystems. https://doi.org/10.1038/s41559-022-01722-1

Bundeswehr (2019). Moorbrand in Meppen. https://www.bundeswehr.de/de/organisation/infrastruktur-umweltschutz-und-dienstleistungen/aktuelles/schwerpunktthemen/moorbrand-in-meppen

Canary Media (2024). Under the sea: Running Tide's ill-fated adventure in ocean carbon removal. https://www.canarymedia.com/articles/carbon-removal/under-the-sea-running-tides-ill-fated-adventure-in-ocean-carbon-removal

Cao et al. (2011). Excessive reliance on afforestation in China's arid and semi-arid regions: Lessons in ecological restoration. https://doi.org/10.1016/j.earscirev.2010.11.002

Carbon Credits (2024). Microsoft Buys Carbon Removal Credits from Grassroots Carbon. https://carboncredits.com/microsoft-buys-carbon-removal-credits-from-grassroots-carbon/

Carbon Gap (2023). Soil Horizons: Unearthing Perspectives on the Future of Soil Carbon Governance – Part 1: A Surface Outlook. https://carbongap.org/wp-content/uploads/2023/10/Carbongap_soil_carbon_governance.pdf

Carbon Herald (2023). Sylvera Wins UK Grant To Research Peatlands CO_2 Removal. https://carbonherald.com/sylvera-wins-uk-grant-to-research-peatlands-co2-removal/

Carbon Herald (2024). Running Tide Shuts Down Citing Lack Of Demand From The Voluntary Market. https://carbonherald.com/running-tide-shuts-down-citing-lack-of-demand-from-the-voluntary-market/

CDR.fyi (2024). https://www.cdr.fyi/

CEEZER (2023). The perks of regenerative agriculture: More than just a carbon sink. https://www.ceezer.earth/insights/the-perks-of-regenerative-agriculture

Corfield (2024). Reflections from the peatland restoration season. https://defraenvironment.blog.gov.uk/2024/05/09/reflections-from-the-peatland-restoration-season/

Counteract (2023). InterEarth. https://counteract.vc/portfolio/inter-earth

Crowther et al. (2015). Mapping tree density at a global scale. https://doi.org/10.1038/nature14967

Davidson et al. (1993). Changes in soil carbon inventories following cultivation of previously untilled soils. https://www.jstor.org/stable/1469217

Energymonitor (2023). Can blue carbon unlock net zero? https://www.energymonitor.ai/tech/carbon-removal/blue-carbon-do-oceans-hold-the-key-to-carbon-removal/

ESG Dive (2024). Microsoft partners with agricultural tech company for carbon removal. https://www.esgdive.com/news/microsoft-partners-with-indigo-ag-for-carbon-removal/719660/

ETH Zurich (2018). Huge grant for ecosystems researcher. https://ethz.ch/en/news-and-events/eth-news/news/2018/02/portrait-tom-crowther.html

ETH Zurich (2019). How trees could help to save the climate. https://ethz.ch/en/news-and-events/eth-news/news/2019/07/how-trees-could-save-the-climate.html

Financial Times (2024). The dubious climate gains of turning soil into a carbon sink. https://www.ft.com/content/91ed3d25-9d5c-4f46-8bd9-23cbb37e1288

Food and Agriculture Organization of the United Nations (2017). The future of food and agriculture: Trends and challenges. https://www.fao.org/3/i6583e/i6583e.pdf

Forbes (2023). Chop Down Forests To Save The Planet? Maybe Not As Crazy As It Sounds. https://www.forbes.com/sites/christopherhelman/2023/07/28/chop-down-forests-to-save-the-planet-maybe-not-as-crazy-as-it-sounds/

Friedlingstein et al. (2019). Comment on "The global tree restoration potential." https://doi.org/10.1126/science.aay8060

Harenda et al. (2018). The Role of Peatlands and Their Carbon Storage Function in the Context of Climate Change. https://www.researchgate.net/publication/321976674_The_Role_of_Peatlands_and_Their_Carbon_Storage_Function_in_the_Context_of_Climate_Change

Heilmayr et al. (2020). Impacts of Chilean forest subsidies on forest cover, carbon and biodiversity. https://doi.org/10.1038/s41893-020-0547-0

Helmholtz Climate Initiative (2022). Climate facts: Why we need peatlands. https://www.helmholtz-klima.de/en/aktuelles/climate-facts-peatlands

History.com (2023). The Juicy 4,000-Year History of Pickles. https://www.history.com/news/pickles-history-timeline

IGB Berlin (2022). Restoration of peatlands: Flooding is not the ideal solution. https://www.igb-berlin.de/en/news/restoration-peatlands-flooding-not-ideal-solution

Institute for Carbon Removal Law and Policy (2018). Carbon Removal Fact Sheet: Blue Carbon. https://www.american.edu/sis/centers/carbon-removal/upload/icrlp_fact_sheet_blue_carbon_181006.pdf

Kenyans.co.ke (2022). Aaron Nanok Named UN Person of the Year. https://www.kenyans.co.ke/news/80868-aaron-nanok-named-un-person-year-2022

Klarna (2023). Supporting high-impact projects. https://www.klarna.com/international/sustainability/climate-solutions/

Lewis et al. (2019). Restoring natural forests is the best way to remove atmospheric carbon. https://doi.org/10.1038/d41586-019-01026-8

Martin et al. (2021). Organic Soils in National Inventory Submissions of EU Countries. https://www.greifswaldmoor.de/files/dokumente/GMC%20Schriften/2021_Martin&Couwenberg.pdf

MIT Technology Review (2022). A stealth effort to bury wood for carbon removal has just raised millions. https://www.technologyreview.com/2022/12/15/1065016/a-stealth-effort-to-bury-wood-for-carbon-removal-has-just-raised-millions/

MIT Technology Review (2022). Running Tide is facing scientist departures and growing concerns over seaweed sinking for carbon removal. https://www.technologyreview.com/2022/06/16/1053758/

running-tide-seaweed-kelp-scientist-departures-ecological-concerns-climate-carbon-removal/

Mo et al. (2023). Integrated global assessment of the natural forest carbon potential. https://doi.org/10.1038/s41586-023-06723-z

Napier (2017). Mangrove project wins Equator Prize. https://www.napier.ac.uk/about-us/news/equator-prize/

Nation (2023). UN honours Kenya's Mikoko Pamoja Mangrove conservation. https://nation.africa/kenya/news/-un-honours-kenya-s-mikoko-pamoja-mangrove-conservation--4412946

S&P Global (2021). Soil carbon credits: The realities on the ground. https://www.spglobal.com/commodityinsights/en/market-insights/blogs/energy-transition/081821-soil-carbon-credits

Science (2023). Farmers are being paid millions to trap carbon in their soils. Will it actually help the planet? https://www.science.org/content/article/farmers-paid-millions-trap-carbon-soils-will-it-actually-help-planet

ScienceNews (2021). Why planting tons of trees isn't enough to solve climate change. https://www.sciencenews.org/article/planting-trees-climate-change-carbon-capture-deforestation

Social Carbon Foundation et al. (2024). Methodology for Peatland Restoration. https://www.socialcarbon.org/scm0010

Spiegel (2018). Meppen: Moorbrand setzt hunderttausende Tonnen CO_2 frei. https://www.spiegel.de/wissenschaft/natur/meppen-moorbrand-setzt-hunderttausende-tonnen-co2-frei-a-1229135.html

State of CDR (2024). The State of Carbon Dioxide Removal – 2nd Edition. https://doi.org/10.17605/OSF.IO/F85QJ

Statista (2023). Agriculture emissions worldwide. https://www.statista.com/topics/10348/agriculture-emissions-worldwide/

The Guardian (2021). 'I've never said we should plant a trillion trees': What ecopreneur Thomas Crowther did next. https://www.theguardian.com/environment/2021/sep/01/ive-never-said-we-should-plant-a-trillion-trees-what-ecopreneur-thomas-crowther-did-next-aoe

The Washington Post (2021). Serious about climate change? Get serious about peat. https://www.washingtonpost.com/world/2021/11/10/cop26-peat-carbon/

Trellis (2024). Deals with Microsoft, Shopify and Stripe fail to keep carbon removal startup alive. https://trellis.net/article/deals-microsoft-shopify-and-stripe-fail-keep-carbon-removal-startup-alive

UK Centre for Ecology & Hydrology (n. d.). Peatland factsheet. https://www.ceh.ac.uk/sites/default/files/Peatland%20factsheet.pdf

United Nations in Kenya (2021). Wawira Njiru Honoured as the 2021 UN Person of the Year. https://kenya.un.org/en/157663-wawira-njiru-honoured-2021-un-person-year

Vox (2020). Tree planting is Trump's politically safe new climate plan. https://www.vox.com/2020/2/4/21123456/sotu-trump-trillion-trees-climate-change

Williamson et al. (2022). Carbon Removal Using Coastal Blue Carbon Ecosystems Is Uncertain and Unreliable, With Questionable Climatic Cost-Effectiveness. https://www.frontiersin.org/articles/10.3389/fclim.2022.853666

Wood et al. (2023). How Blue Carbon Can Tackle the Climate, Biodiversity and Development Crises. https://www.wri.org/insights/what-is-blue-carbon-benefits-for-people-planet

World Resources Institute (2023). Blue Carbon Handbook Launch. https://www.youtube.com/watch?v=K0yaq2fkNuY

Yale Environment Review (2021). Changing the conversation around soil carbon. https://environment-review.yale.edu/changing-conversation-around-soil-carbon

You et al. (2024). Net greenhouse gas balance in U. S. croplands: How can soils be part of the climate solution? https://doi.org/10.1111/gcb.17109

Chapter 5

Beerling et al. (2020). Potential for large-scale CO_2 removal via enhanced rock weathering with croplands. https://doi.org/10.1038/s41586-020-2448-9

Bioenergy International (2024). EBI releases annual European Biochar Market Report. https://bioenergyinternational.com/ebi-releases-annual-european-biochar-market-report/

Carbon Herald (2023). Frontier Makes Largest Carbon Removal Purchase From Lithos Carbon. https://carbonherald.com/frontier-makes-largest-carbon-removal-purchase-from-lithos-carbon/

Carbon to Sea Initiative (2023). The promise of ocean-based carbon removal. https://carbontosea.org/

CDR.fyi (2024). https://www.cdr.fyi/

CDR.fyi (2024). 2024 Q3 Durable CDR Market Update. https://www.cdr.fyi/blog/2024-q3-durable-cdr-market-update-time-to-build-the-base

CEEZER (2023). Enhanced rock weathering. https://25308917.fs1.hubspotusercontent-eu1.net/hubfs/25308917/03_Whitepaper/Enhanced_Weathering_final.pdf

CEEZER (2023). How biochar emerged as an unexpected champion in the fight against the climate crisis. https://www.ceezer.earth/insights/how-biochar-emerged-as-an-unexpected-champion-in-the-fight-against-the-climate-crisis

Coastal Review (2022). Carbon capture project proposed for ocean waters off Duck. https://coastalreview.org/2022/11/carbon-capture-project-proposed-for-ocean-waters-off-duck/

Ebb Carbon (2023). Meet Ebb Carbon. https://www.ebbcarbon.com/meet-ebb-carbon

Gruber et al. (2019). The oceanic sink for anthropogenic CO_2 from 1994 to 2007. https://doi.org/10.1126/science.aau5153

Heatmap (2023). There Will Soon Be More Concrete Than Biomass on Earth. https://heatmap.news/economy/the-planet-s-jaw-dropping-astonishing-downright-shocking-amount-of-concrete

Heatmap (2024). The First Open Ocean Carbon Removal Project in the U. S. Just Got a Green Light. https://heatmap.news/technology/ocean-carbon-removal-vesta

International Maritime Organization (2020). Fourth IMO Greenhouse Gas Study. https://wwwcdn.imo.org/localresources/en/OurWork/Environment/Documents/Fourth%20IMO%20GHG%20Study%202020%20-%20Full%20report%20and%20annexes.pdf

IPCC (2023). Climate Change 2023: Synthesis Report. Contribution of Working Groups I, II and III to the Sixth Assessment Report of the Intergovernmental Panel on Climate Change. https://doi.org/10.59327/IPCC/AR6-9789291691647

Klarna (2022). Klarna partners with Ireland-based Silicate to remove CO_2 emissions and maximize positive climate impact. https://www.klarna.com/international/press/klarna-partners-with-ireland-based-silicate-to-remove-co2-emissions-and-maximize-positive-climate-impact/

MIT Technology Review (2020). How green sand could capture billions of tons of carbon dioxide. https://www.technologyreview.com/2020/06/22/1004218/how-green-sand-could-capture-billions-of-tons-of-carbon-dioxide/

Reuters (2022). Stripe, Shopify commit $11 million to carbon removal projects. https://www.reuters.com/business/sustainable-business/stripe-shopify-commit-11-million-carbon-removal-projects-2022-12-15/

Sharma et al. (2022). Will open waste burning become India's largest air pollution source? https://doi.org/10.1016/j.envpol.2021.118310

State of CDR (2024). The State of Carbon Dioxide Removal – 2nd Edition. https://doi.org/10.17605/OSF.IO/F85QJ

Supercritical (2023). Biochar. https://gosupercritical.com/carbon-removal/biochar

Supercritical (2024). Boom or Bust? 2024 Biochar Market Outlook. https://climate.gosupercritical.com/biochar-report/

Tagesschau (2018). Abschied von der Steinkohle: Ingo Zamperoni live aus dem Pott. https://www.youtube.com/watch?v=sXQ5vB2qQs0

Vesta (2023). Watch Vesta in Solving for Zero. https://www.vesta.earth/

Webb et al. (2021). Removing Carbon Dioxide Through Ocean Alkalinity Enhancement: Legal Challenges and Opportunities. https://scholarship.law.columbia.edu/faculty_scholarship/2739/

Ye et al. (2020). Biochar effects on crop yields with and without fertilizer: A meta-analysis of field studies using separate controls. https://doi.org/10.1111/sum.12546

Zeng et al. (2022). Natural and Anthropogenic Driving Forces of Carbonate Weathering and the Related Carbon Sink Flux: A Model Comparison Study at Global Scale. https://doi.org/10.1029/2021GB007096

Chapter 6

1PointFive (2022). 1PointFive announces agreement with Airbus for the purchase of 400,000 tonnes of carbon removal credits. https://www.globenewswire.com/news-release/2022/03/17/2405660/0/en/1PointFive-announces-agreement-with-Airbus-for-the-purchase-of-400-000-tonnes-of-carbon-removal-credits.html

1PointFive (2024). 1PointFive Announces Agreement to Sell 500,000 Metric Tons of Direct Air Capture Carbon Removal Credits to Microsoft. https://www.globenewswire.com/news-release/2024/07/09/2910312/0/en/1PointFive-Announces-Agreement-to-Sell-500-000-Metric-Tons-of-Direct-Air-Capture-Carbon-Removal-Credits-to-Microsoft.html

BBC (2022). Drax: UK power station owner cuts down primary forests in Canada. https://www.bbc.com/news/science-environment-63089348

CarbonX (2024). CDR Market Quarterly Review 02.2024. https://pitch.com/v/q2-2024-review-3vsh8f/9500ec48-f301-4094-9c2f-7a5a162f2478

CDR.fyi (2023). List of known CDR purchases. https://docs.google.com/spreadsheets/d/1BH_B_Df_7e2l6AH8_8a0aK70nlAJXfCTwfyCgxkL5C8/edit?usp=drive_web&ouid=108589226295607605414

Climeworks (2023). BCG and Climeworks sign 15-year partnership agreement. https://climeworks.com/press-release/bcg-and-climeworks-sign-15-year-partnership-agreement

Climeworks (2023). J. P. Morgan Chase and Climeworks. https://climeworks.com/press-release/jp-morgan-chase-signs-landmark-cdr-agreement-with-climeworks

Climeworks (2024). Support the scale-up of carbon removal. https://climeworks.com/subscriptions

CNBC (2023). J. P. Morgan agrees to purchase $200 million worth of carbon removal. https://www.cnbc.com/2023/05/23/jpmorgan-agrees-to-purchase-200-million-worth-of-carbon-removal.html

Drax (2019). Drax sets world-first ambition to become carbon negative by 2030. https://www.drax.com/press_release/drax-sets-world-first-ambition-to-become-carbon-negative-by-2030/

Drax (2021). Annual report and accounts 2020. https://www.drax.com/wp-content/uploads/2021/03/Drax_AR2020.pdf

Drax (2024). Drax announces carbon removals deal with Karbon-X. https://www.drax.com/press_release/drax-announces-carbon-removals-deal-with-karbon-x/

Drewelies, M. (2023). Credit prices vary heavily by technology. Not always by quality.

EASAC (2022). "Look before you Leap": European Science Academies Caution against Subsidies for Bioenergy with Carbon Capture and Storage (BECCS). https://easac.eu/news/details/look-before-you-leap-european-science-academies-cau

tion-against-subsidies-for-bioenergy-with-carbon-capture-and-storage-beccs/

Energymonitor (2022). Can BECCS be saved from the net-zero scrapheap? https://www.energymonitor.ai/carbon-removal/can-beccs-be-saved-from-the-net-zero-scrapheap/

ESG Today (2024). Microsoft Signs 1 Million Tonne Bioenergy-based Carbon Removal Agreement with Ørsted. https://www.esgtoday.com/microsoft-signs-1-million-tonne-bioenergy-based-carbon-removal-agreement-with-orsted/

ESG Today (2024). Microsoft Signs Largest-Ever 3.3 Million Tonne Carbon Removal Deal with Stockholm Exergi. https://www.esgtoday.com/microsoft-signs-largest-ever-3-3-million-tonne-carbon-removal-deal-with-stockholm-exergi/

Financial Times (2024). UK power stations burnt wood from old forest areas, Drax emails show. https://www.ft.com/content/34550e7d-9d65-4756-8ffa-53f821dd14d0

Frontier (2023). Apply to be a Frontier supplier. https://frontierclimate.com/apply

Frontier (2024). Frontier's carbon removal portfolio. https://frontierclimate.com/portfolio

German Federal Ministry for Economic Affairs and Climate (2024). Cabinet clears path for CCS in Germany. https://www.bmwk.de/Redaktion/EN/Pressemitteilungen/2024/05/20240529-cabinet-clears-path-for-ccs-in-germany.html

Google (2024). Our first-of-its-kind direct air capture deal forges a path to lower costs. https://blog.google/outreach-initiatives/sustainability/google-holocene-direct-air-capture/

IEA (2021). Northern Lights – CCUS around the world in 2021 – Analysis. https://www.iea.org/reports/ccus-around-the-world-in-2021/northern-lights

IEA (2023). Bioenergy with Carbon Capture and Storage. https://www.iea.org/energy-system/carbon-capture-utilisation-and-storage/bioenergy-with-carbon-capture-and-storage

IEA (2024). CCUS Projects Database. https://www.iea.org/data-and-statistics/data-product/ccus-projects-database

IPCC (2023). Mitigation Pathways Compatible with Long-term Goals. https://doi.org/10.1017/9781009157926.005

Merchant, N. (2023). Digging deep on carbon storage – Jack Andreasen and Dr. Claire Nelson. https://carboncurve.substack.com/p/digging-deep-on-carbon-storage

MIT (2016). Carbon Capture and Sequestration Technologies. https://sequestration.mit.edu/tools/projects/sleipner.html

Nature (2021). Concrete needs to lose its colossal carbon footprint. https://doi.org/10.1038/d41586-021-02612-5

Net Zero Tracker (2024). Stockholm. https://zerotracker.net/cities/stockholm-cit-0136

OGE (2022). OGE and TES join forces to develop a 1,000 km CO_2 transmission system. https://oge.net/en/press-releases/2022/oge-and-tes-join-forces-to-develop-a-1-000-km-co-2-transmission-system

OMR (2022). OMR #521 mit Climeworks-Gründer Christoph Gebald (521). https://omr.com/de/daily/omr-podcast-christoph-gebald-climeworks

Politico (2022). Stockholm bets on carbon capture to hit net zero. https://www.politico.eu/article/stockholm-bet-carbon-capture-hit-net-zero-target-climate-crisis/

Raz, G. (2022). How I Built this Lab! Climeworks – Jan Wurzbacher (423). https://podcasts.apple.com/de/podcast/hibt-lab-climeworks-jan-wurzbacher/id1150510297?i=1000567426551

Reuters (2023). Amazon makes first investment in direct air capture climate technology. https://www.reuters.com/business/environment/amazon-makes-first-investment-direct-air-capture-climate-technology-2023-09-12/

Reuters (2023). Burning questions surround biomass-based carbon removals. https://www.reuters.com/sustainability/climate-energy/burning-questions-surround-biomass-based-removals-2023-10-23/

Reuters (2023). How Iceland's Carbfix is harnessing the power of turning CO_2 into stone. https://www.reuters.com/sustainability/climate-energy/how-icelands-carbfix-is-harnessing-power-turning-co2-into-stone-2023-10-30/

Reuters (2023). Occidental buys carbon air capture tech firm for $1.1 billion. https://www.reuters.com/markets/deals/occidental-petroleum-buy-carbon-engineering-11-bln-2023-08-15/

Sievert at al. (2024). Considering technology characteristics to project future costs of direct air capture. https://doi.org/10.1016/j.joule.2024.02.005

State of CDR (2024). The State of Carbon Dioxide Removal – 2nd Edition. https://doi.org/10.17605/OSF.IO/F85QJ

The Energy Mix (2023). Occidental Seeks '60, 70, 80 Years' of Oil Extraction with Carbon Engineering Buyout. https://www.theenergymix.com/occidental-seeks-60-70-80-years-of-oil-extraction-with-carbon-engineering-buyout/

The Guardian (2021). From pollutant to product: The companies making stuff from CO_2. https://www.theguardian.com/environment/2021/dec/05/carbon-dioxide-co2-capture-utilisation-products-vodka-jet-fuel-protein

The Guardian (2021). Green groups dispute power station claim that biomass is carbon-neutral. https://www.theguardian.com/business/2021/mar/23/green-groups-dispute-power-station-claim-biomass-carbon-neutral

The Guardian (2023). The world's biggest carbon capture facility is being built in Texas. Will it work? https://www.theguardian.com/environment/2023/sep/12/carbon-capture-texas-worlds-biggest-will-it-work

Trove Research (2023). BECCS – promising technology for net zero or an expensive bet? https://trove-research.com/report/beccs-promising-technology-for-net-zero-or-an-expensive-bet

Chapter 7

Axios Generate (2024). Facebook parent Meta leaves carbon coalition. https://www.axios.com/newsletters/axios-generate-bc353380-65f9-11ef-b70e-99d40e15156d.html

Bloomberg (2022). Junk Carbon Offsets Are What Make These Big Companies Carbon Neutral. https://www.bloomberg.com/graphics/2022-carbon-offsets-renewable-energy/

Carbon Market Watch (2024). Trading in hot air: Why a market in temporary carbon removals is a bad idea. https://carbonmarketwatch.org/2024/10/03/trading-in-hot-air-why-a-market-in-temporary-carbon-removals-is-a-bad-idea/

Carbon Trust (2024). Carbon neutral verification. https://www.carbontrust.com/what-we-do/product-carbon-footprint-labelling/carbon-neutral-verification

CDR.fyi (2024). https://www.cdr.fyi/leaderboards

CDR.fyi (2024). 2024 Q2 Durable CDR Market Update. https://www.cdr.fyi/blog/2024-q2-durable-cdr-market-update-microsoft-market-maker

Frontier (2023). An advance market commitment to accelerate carbon removal. https://frontierclimate.com/

HBS Working Knowledge – Climate Rising (2023). Transcript: Going Carbon Negative at Microsoft. https://www.hbs.edu/environment/podcast/Pages/podcast-details.aspx?episode=7332431994

Microsoft Blog (2021). One Year Later: The Path to Carbon Negative. https://blogs.microsoft.com/blog/2021/01/28/one-year-later-the-path-to-carbon-negative-a-progress-report-on-our-climate-moonshot/

Persefoni (2024). AB 1305 Explained: Navigating California's Voluntary Carbon Markets Disclosures. https://www.persefoni.com/blog/ab-1305

Science Based Targets (2019). 1.5°C vs. 2°C: A World of Difference. https://sciencebasedtargets.org/blog/1-5-c-vs-2-c-a-world-of-difference

Science Based Targets (2023). Beyond Value Chain Mitigation. https://sciencebasedtargets.org/beyond-value-chain-mitigation

South Pole (2023). South Pole Calls for Businesses to Align Around New Future-Proof Green Claim Funding Climate Action. https://www.southpole.com/news/south-pole-calls-for-businesses-to-align-around-new-future-proof-green-claim-funding-climate-action#:~:text=London%2C%20June%2027%2C%202023%20%E2%80%93,and%20beyond%20their%20value%20chain

Swiss Re (2022). Our CO_2 Net Zero Programme. https://www.swissre.com/sustainability/sustainable-operations/co2netzero-programme.html

The Guardian (2023). Delta Air Lines Lawsuit Over Carbon Neutrality. https://www.theguardian.com/environment/2023/may/30/delta-air-lines-lawsuit-carbon-neutrality-aoe

Chapter 8

Accountancy Europe (2022). Mandatory rotation of auditors. https://www.accountancyeurope.eu/wp-content/uploads/2022/12/Audit-Rotation-2022_Accountancy_EU.pdf

Arizona Daily Star (1986). Lake Nyos Disaster. https://blog.newspapers.com/lake-nyos-disaster-august-21-1986/

atmosfair (2023). Offset your flight. https://www.atmosfair.de/en/offset/flight/

Carbon180 (2021). Removing Forward. https://static1.squarespace.com/static/5b9362d89d5abb8c51d474f8/t/6115485ae47e7f00829083e1/1628784739915/ Carbon180+RemovingForward.pdf

Carbon Wrangler (2023). We Know What to Do on Climate. https://carbonwrangler.medium.com/we-know-what-to-do-on-climate-d448c9e1f9c2

CATF (2023). Europe's cross-border CO_2 networks start to take shape. https://www.catf.us/2023/02/europes-cross-border-co2-networks-start-to-take-shape/

Clarion Ledger (2020). 'Foaming at the mouth': First responders describe scene after pipeline rupture, gas leak. https://eu.clarionledger.com/story/news/local/2020/02/27/yazoo-county-pipe-rupture-co-2-gas-leak-firstresponders-rescues/4871726002/

Clean Air Task Force (2023). Fact Sheet: Carbon Capture and the Inflation Reduction Act. https://www.catf.us/resource/carbon-capture-inflation-reduction-act/

DOE (2023). DOE Announces \$35 Million to Accelerate Carbon Dioxide Removal. https://www.energy.gov/fecm/articles/doe-announces-35-million-accelerate-carbon-dioxide-removal

E&E News (2023). False Promise: Carbon Removal Plans Rankle Community Advocates. https://www.eenews.net/articles/false-promise-does-carbon-removal-plans-rankle-community-advocates/

EnArgus (2023). CO_2-Speicherung. https://www.enargus.de/pub/bscw.cgi/d1927-2/*/*/CO2-Speicherung.html?op=Wiki.getwiki

Energy4Climate (2022). Impuls: Nationaler Planungsprozess für eine CO_2-Transportinfrastruktur. https://www.energy4climate.nrw/aktuelles/newsroom/aufbau-einer-infrastruktur-fuer-den-transport-von-kohlendioxid-was-gilt-es-zu-beruecksichtigen-ein-impuls

Figueiredo et al. (2006). The Liability of Carbon Dioxide Storage. https://sequestration.mit.edu/pdf/GHGT8_deFigueiredo.pdf

Frontier (2023). An advance market commitment to accelerate carbon removal. https://frontierclimate.com/

Government of Canada (2024). Government of Canada commits to purchase carbon dioxide removal services to green government operations and achieve net-zero emissions. https://www.canada.ca/en/treasury-board-secretariat/news/2024/10/government-of-canada-commits-to-purchase-carbon-dioxide-removal-services-to-green-government-operations-and-achieve-net-zero-emissions.html

Greenpeace UNEARTHED (2022). 'How are we going to live?' Families dispossessed of their land to make way for Total's Congo offsetting project. https://unearthed.greenpeace.org/2022/12/12/total-congo-offsetting-land-dispossessed/

Nemet, G. (2019). How Solar Became Cheap. https://www.howsolargotcheap.com/

NPR (2021). Elon Musk Funds $100 Million XPRIZE For Pursuit Of New Carbon Removal Ideas. https://www.npr.org/2021/02/08/965372754/elon-musk-funds-100-million-xprize-for-pursuit-of-new-carbon-removal-ideas

Our World in Data (2023). CO_2 Emissions Per Capita. https://ourworldindata.org/grapher/co-emissions-per-capita

Pipeline Safety Trust (2023). Carbon Dioxide Pipelines: Dangerous and Under-Regulated. https://pstrust.org/carbon-dioxide-pipelines-dangerous-and-under-regulated/

Protocol (2022). Carbon Removal Cost Per Ton. https://www.protocol.com/bulletins/carbon-removal-cost-per-ton

Reuters (2022). Global carbon markets value surged to record $851 bln last year – Refinitiv. https://www.reuters.com/business/energy/global-carbon-markets-value-surged-record-851-bln-last-year-refinitiv-2022-01-31/

Science Based Targets (2019). 1.5°C vs. 2°C: A World of Difference. https://sciencebasedtargets.org/blog/1-5-c-vs-2-c-a-world-of-difference

Science Based Targets (2023). Beyond Value Chain Mitigation. https://sciencebasedtargets.org/beyond-value-chain-mitigation

South Pole (2023). South Pole calls for businesses to align around new future-proof green claim: Funding Climate Action. https://

www.southpole.com/news/south-pole-calls-for-businesses-to-align-around-new-future-proof-green-claim-funding-climate-action

Epilogue

Boston Consulting Group (2023). The Time for Carbon Removal Has Come. https://web-assets.bcg.com/67/f7/0f41cd074a66b49cdb8baf5e59c0/bcg-the-time-for-carbon-removal-has-come-sep-2023-r.pdf

Boston Consulting Group (2024). Europe and Germany's Role in Catalyzing a Trillion-Euro Industry. https://assets.foleon.com/eu-central-1/de-uploads-7e3kk3/50809/240620_dvne_bcg_cdr_economic_potential_en_vfinal_180dpi.b4aa840efcaf.pdf?utm_description=organic

CDR.fyi (2022). CDR.fyi 2022 Year in Review. https://medium.com/cdr-fyi/cdr-fyi-2022-year-in-review-d095acd9a1a0

CDR.fyi (2024). 2024 Q2 Durable CDR Market Update. https://www.cdr.fyi/blog/2024-q2-durable-cdr-market-update-microsoft-market-maker

Höglund, R. (2023). Only 0.5% of Companies with SBTi Targets Are Pursuing Carbon Removal. https://marginalcarbon.substack.com/p/only-05-of-companies-with-sbti-targets?publication_id=1257586&post_id=137249512&isFreemail=true&r=2qbuw6

State of CDR (2024). The State of Carbon Dioxide Removal – 2nd Edition. https://doi.org/10.17605/OSF.IO/F85QJ

US EPA (2024). Inventory of U.S. Greenhouse Gas Emissions and Sinks. https://www.epa.gov/ghgemissions/inventory-us-greenhouse-gas-emissions-and-sinks

ABOUT THE AUTHORS

Marian Krüger is the founder and director of remove, an organization that supports European, Indian, and African carbon removal start-ups. Previously, the behavioural economist headed the Sustainability in Business Lab at ETH Zurich, advised industrial companies and public institutions on decarbonization and founded a successful solar start-up.

Dr. Benedict Probst leads the Net Zero Lab at the Max Planck Institute for Innovation and Competition and is a Fellow of Cambridge University. Previously, the environmental economist worked in the Group for Sustainability and Technology at ETH Zurich. His research has appeared in leading journals such as *Nature Sustainability* and various media outlets.